Contents

D1547827

Foreword

In every age the Christian faces specific and sometimes unique challenges to his faith.

The Western world has seen a massive resurgence of interest in the occult, and particularly astrology. This has been especially true of students. Part of the explanation can be found in the fact that students are increasingly aware that science can tell us how the universe functions but not why, and they have experienced firsthand in an affluent society that "man cannot live by bread alone." In our time astrology has gained enormous prominence and has become a competitor to Christianity and, in some instances, an attractive fellow traveler among some naive Christians.

It is important for Christians, particularly students in their time and generation, to understand the background, appeal and the fallacies of the astrological phenomenon. The reason for this is twofold: First, he must be preserved from being engulfed by it himself and, second, he should be in a position to help those who have become entangled in it to see through it and come to the one who is "the Way, the Truth, and the Life" and the one who can give us clear guidance and insight into the future.

Stars, Signs, and Salvation in the Age of Aquarius will shed considerable light on this important subject. The reader will gain the historical perspective of astrology and will be able to see how we have arrived at the current high tide.

More important, he will be able to see through the claims of many astrologers that the Bible supports this philosophy, and he will be made aware that, in fact, the Scriptures emphatically oppose those who claim to know the future or who ascribe power over men to heavenly bodies. It will give him material that will enable him to formulate thoughtful questions to the adherent of astrology as well as to divert him from the temptation to imbibe himself. The book is both timely and useful. Many will profit from its study and use.

Paul E. Little

Introduction

> Tribal man is tightly sealed in an integral collective
> awareness that transcends conventional boundaries
> of time and space. As such, the new society will be
> one mythic integration, a resonating world akin to the
> old tribal chamber where magic will live again: a
> world of ESP. The current interest of youth in astrol-
> ogy, clairvoyance and the occult is no coincidence.
> —Marshall McLuhan

Astrology today rides upon a crest of popularity
unequaled in its history. The traditional rhyme:

"The Ram, the Bull, the Heavenly Twins,
And next the Crab the Lion shines,
    The Virgin and the Scales,
The Scorpion, Archer, and Sea-Goat,
The Man that bears the Watering-Pot,
    The Fish with glittering tails."

depicts for us the symbols of the zodiac which have
become household terms. Of course they depict
the traditional 12 constellations. Recently Steven
Schmidt published a book, *Astrology 14,* in which he
points out that "there are now 14 constellations oc-
cupying the belt of the Zodiac." Schmidt has added
Cetus the Whale, and Ophichus the Serpent slayer.
There are others who admit to only 8 or 10 constellations, while some have set forth a zodiac of 24
constellations.

The word zodiac is derived from the ancient Greek
word *zodiakos,* meaning (a circle) "of animals." The
word astrology is derived from two Greek words
astra meaning "star" and *logos* meaning "word."
Thus astrology is the word or science of the stars.

Astrology is taking the Western world by storm.

Mankind has launched himself into a mystical orbit, where hopefully some answers to life's enigmas can be encountered. In the United States alone, it has been estimated that over 40 million people dabble in astrology.

Today syndicated newspaper columns of horoscopes and other astrological information appear in the vast majority of our newspapers. Even those who frown upon astrology cannot resist looking at their horoscopes to see what the day will bring. Magazines, paperback books, slot-machines, computers, etc., are all part of the mass media which sets astrology in the forefront of the public. Astrologers are available for personal consultation. In 1969, the New York Abraham & Straus department store retained Lloyd Cope as its official astrological consultant. Opportunities to learn in astrological workshops, high school and college courses on various aspects of astrology, schools on astrology (e.g., the First Temple and College of Astrology in Los Angeles), and even home study courses, such as Sybil Leek's *How To Be Your Own Astrologer,* are available. "What's My Sign" was the name of a popular astrology panel show.

It is purported that astrology has ramifications for so many different areas of life, including diet, health, sex, marriage, career, politics, etc. As *McCall's* reports: "For many of today's young, astrology has taken the place of psychology as the personality decoder of their generation." According to Sally Kempton, parents are even planning the birth of their children under favorable signs, and for those interested, a book *Your Baby's First Horoscope* is available. One can even obtain horoscopes for one's dog, e.g., Lester Belt's *Your Dog's Astrological Horoscope.* (There is also a *Cat Horoscope Book.*) One of the most popular volumes presently is *Astrology and Horseracing.*

Business has found astrology to be very profitable. Besides the scores of paperback books available, retail stores sell a host of items from stationery and paper napkins to furniture embellished with the various signs of the zodiac.

Several astrological associations have been formed, e.g., the International Committee of Humanistic Astrology (developed to provide a person-oriented approach to astrology), the American Federation of Astrologers, the New England Astrological Association, and the International Scientific Astrological Research Association. Several magazines, including *American Astrology* and *Astrological Digest,* have also come into existence.

Many current religious movements focusing upon astrology in their beliefs—Rosicrucianism, Theosophy, I Ching, Edgar Cayce and the Association for Research and Enlightenment, etc.—have come into current prominence because of the rise of astrology in America.

Astrology today is enjoying heights of popularity never before realized in its long history, and its future appears to be even brighter, according to McLuhan and others; but, is it the answer to the despair and dilemma of modern man? And has it been the answer throughout history?

I

The Nature and History of Astrology

In this age of miraculous technology which is advancing much more rapidly than the most imaginative science-fiction writer can conceive, in this age of man's new "tribalism," [1] in this age of man's new "infantilization," [2] in this Aquarian Age (as the cultists, including astrologers, call our new age), in this second industrial revolution—millions of people from all walks of life and in almost every, if not every, corner, nation, and tribe of the earth are turning "to the stars" [3] for guidance in every phase of life— health, choice of mate, diet, business, investments, occupation, hobbies, or you name it!

In America alone you can scarcely find a newspaper without its astrological guidance column. Some forty million Americans dabble in this occult, magical, pseudo-science. Even television stations have found astrological horoscopes, originally placed in station breaks, so popular that astrologers have been hired to produce weekly half-hour programs. Astrological publications have soared to new heights in popularity. Just look at the paperbacks alone devoted to the subject at your favorite bookstore or note the ever increasing volume of new astrological books being published in hard cover, not to mention the numerous reprints of older astrological "classics." Circulation and sales of periodicals devoted wholly or in part to astrology have soared to fantastic proportions. In France, for instance, one of these magazines alone has a circulation of around four hundred thousand.

The resurgence of this ancient form of divination—of foretelling the future—has created a new multi-million, perhaps multi-billion, dollar industry. Since not only the untrained, ignorant peoples of the world, but also persons with excellent educational backgrounds, are turning to this ancient superstition[4]—in fact it has even penetrated the Christian church—intelligent, alert, interested Christians need to acquire a knowledge of this old art and become prepared in this area to earnestly "contend for the faith which was once delivered unto the saints." [5]

Although astrology has far more devotees than astronomy and shares a common origin with it, the claim which modern astrologers and devotees of the cult often make—namely, that astrology is far more ancient than astronomy—is very misleading, and is, at best, a half (or less) truth! The term (word) *astrology* may be older than the term *astronomy,* but the original meaning of astrology was "the word(s) of the star(s)," exactly what the component parts of the word signify. For centuries, even millennia, the word, astrology, did not convey its modern signification of forecasting the future for individuals. Instead it accurately described early man's intense interest in his heavenly surroundings, and his appreciation of the "great, magnificent, and immutable" handiwork of the only true Creator-God. Only gradually did it begin to acquire the features which today characterize astrology, and then only as an additional acquired meaning, retaining as its prime meaning the original signification.

The Nature of Modern Astrology

Before briefly tracing the history of the origin of modern astrology, of the complete divorce of its two major divisions (natural and juridical) into astronomy and non-astronomical astrology, and of its severance from man's interest in his heavenly surroundings and of his appreciation for God's magnificent, omnipotent, creative works in the universe, a cursory examination of the nature of modern astrology is advisable. Astrology is rooted in many false premises and assumptions, such as the false belief that the sun, moon, and planets revolve around the earth as their center, and the equally erroneous, pagan concept that some external, impersonal force(s) control(s) or strongly influence(s) man.[6]

To envision the astrologer's universe of "stars," take any spherical object, for example, a volley ball. With a magic marker, draw a thin complete circle around its middle (use black colored ink for this circle). Select a different color marker with a very broad tip. Assuming that you select red this time, draw a very broad red circle around the middle of the ball again. This second circle must intersect the first one and must lie elsewhere only a little above and a little below the first black thin-lined circle. Imagine the center of the ball to be the earth; the thin black circle then represents the imaginary, "celestial equator" (the earth's equator extended to the heavens) and the thick red circle the "zodiac." The center of the red circle pictures the ecliptic, the apparent course of the sun as it appears to rotate around the earth during the course of a solar year. The red circle was purposely drawn very wide or broad so that it could stand for the longer, apparent periodic paths[7] of the wandering "stars" around the earth.

Next divide the red circle into twelve equal parts; the circle then represents the astrologer's zodiac. This term, the *zodiac*,[8] comes from a Greek word meaning "to do with animals." The latter word in turn comes from a word meaning "a small painted or carved animal." The plural form was used by Aristotle to denote the twelve divisions of the celestial ecliptic, probably because many of the divisions were given the names of animals. Each of the divisions corresponds to one of the twelve constellations lying around the celestial zodiac: Aries (the Ram), Taurus (the Bull), Gemini (the Twins), Cancer (the Crab), Leo (the Lion), Virgo (the Virgin), Libra (the Scales), Scorpio (the Scorpion), Sagittarius (the Archer), Capricorn (the Goat), Aquarius (the Water-bearer), and Pisces (the Fishes).

A distinction must be made, however, between the twelve heavenly constellations and the twelve signs of the zodiac, even though both bear the same set of names. The astrologer's signs are not identical with the celestial constellations. In fact, today whenever an astrologer states that you are born under a certain sign, he does *not* mean that you are born under that actual constellation with that particular name. Likewise, he does not mean that the sun appears to be in that constellation in its apparent, annual course through the celestial zodiac. At one time the latter statement would have been true, but, due to the "precession of the equinoxes" (a very slow event, caused by the wobbling of the earth on its axis, taking 25,800 years to complete its cycle), the sun no longer appears to be in the constellation bearing the same name as the astrological sign—it now is in another constellation (at least it appears to be). This shift of the zodiac for a complete sign-constellation is conveniently ignored by astrologers today— a fact which gives telling ammunition for those who violently oppose astrology!

The volley ball with its two circles—black and red—and with the twelve equal divisions of the wide red circle gives you a graphic picture of the astrological universe. It is a geocentric universe—i.e., it views the universe with the earth being the center and with the ten[9] mobile planets moving about the earth through the twelve signs of the zodiac, as depicted by the wide red circle. These wandering bodies are believed to have (or to reveal) important influences, if not control, upon the lives of nations and of individuals. To determine the influence of these "stars" upon the life of some person, a horoscope,[10] so astrologers maintain, must be constructed. To construct, or cast a horoscope the exact time and place of birth must be known. The horoscope then graphically portrays the astrological "location" of the stars for a given individual or nation at that time and place of his birth.

There exist many different ways of representing the astrological horoscope with all its data. One simple method[11] is to take a plain, white, 8-1/2 x 11 sheet of paper and to draw three concentric circles upon it. The first circle has a diameter of one and one-half inches, the second of six inches, and the third of six and one-half inches. These circles are divided into four quarters by drawing two perpendicular diameters, one vertical and the other horizontal. Each quarter-circle is further subdivided into three equal portions by drawing appropriate diameters. The twelve spaces inside the first circle are now numbered consecutively from one to twelve by beginning with the space on the left just below the horizontal diameter and proceeding in a counter-clockwise direction. The twelve spaces of the three circles correspond to the twelve houses of the horoscope.

Although astrologers use different systems of houses, in each system the houses (like the ones you have constructed) are fixed. The twelve signs of the zodiac which must be placed in the horoscope you are constructing are not fixed; they vary according to the time of the year at which you were born. Hence these houses must not be confused with either the heavenly constellations nor with the astrological signs, even though there are twelve of each.

In the space between circles two or three, the names, symbols, or both, of the astrological signs are placed in a counter-clockwise direction beginning with house number one. In it you place the astrological sign which was rising at the exact time of your birth; in the next house the next sign, following the order given above. You proceed in this manner until each house has been assigned to its appropriated sign. Thus if you were born on October 30, you would have been born under the astrological sign of Scorpio. Suppose that your rising sign was also Scorpio and that the ascendent is 6^0 15'. Hence in the space between circles two and three in house number one, you would place Scorpio or its symbol ♏ and note 6^0 15'.

In house number two you would place Sagittarius (♐), and so forth, until you had placed in house number twelve the sign of Libra (♎). The twelve spaces between circles one and two are frequently split in half by the use of segments of radii or diameters. In these twelve or twenty-four spaces are placed the eleven astrological stars or planets. Beside them are put numbers so that the "exact" location can be known. Astrologers always use symbols instead of names for these planets. This data permits the interpreter of the horoscope to determine the favorable or unfavorable aspects of their relationship to one another. This relationship the astrologer calls "aspects."

The bad aspects are called opposition and square. They occur in a horoscope when two planets are separated by 180^0 or 90^0, respectively (a full circle representing 360^0). The good aspects are sextile and trine (this last one is an especially good aspect); these occur when two planets are separated by 60^0 or 120^0, respectively. The remaining aspect is neither good nor bad; its nature depends on the nature of the two planets which are very close together, within 8^0-10^0 of one another. When this occurs, the two planets are said to be in conjunction with one another.

Anyone with normal intelligence, with the assistance of the prepared astrological tables and some oral or written instruction, can learn to cast a horoscope, but its interpretation is an entirely different matter. As can be seen from the nature of the planetary aspects, interpretation is very complex. It requires knowledge not only of the significance of these aspects and of the houses, but also a thorough understanding of the nature of each sign and of each star as well as all of the intricate interrelationships.

Modern horoscopes may be used for many purposes; the more important are: (1) genethliacal astrology which deals with all aspects of interpreting and casting individual horoscopes; (2) mundane astrology which is concerned with the fortunes of the state; and (3) horary astrology which uses horoscopes to answer questions as they arise. Astrology is used for many other purposes, such as medical astrology and electional astrology—i.e., the use of horoscopes to determine the most opportune moment for undertaking some enterprise.

Certain interesting conclusions may be drawn from the astrological process; for example, there should exist astrological "fraternal" and "identical" twins, corresponding to the physical fraternal and identical twins. Astrologically identical twins would have the same, or nearly so, birth places and times, the latter being the most important to be exactly the same. Astrologers and their devotees have been quick to recognize this conclusion, and they are not reluctant to cite all varieties of famous (and sometimes not so famous) examples. They frequently cite some instances in which these "twins" share some common events in time, e.g., death, illnesses, and the like.

To appreciate the difficulties of interpreting the date of the horoscope just read the various predictions[12] that prominent astrologers have made for the coming year. By making comparisons of them, you will note not only similarities but also striking differences—plus considerable vagueness. Consequently it is not at all surprising that astrology has been described vividly and aptly as a divinational game which is "played with symbols called stars and planets on a board called the Zodiac. It is as far removed from realities as a game of Monopoly is from transactions of the Chase Manhattan Bank." [13] It is a form of magic which has survived for about two thousand years and is today being presented in a secular form stripped apparently naked of all its magical and pagan origins and foundations. Astrology is a natural result of fallen man's attempt to understand his surroundings, and of his determination not to worship or acknowledge the one, true God.

The History and Origins of Astronomy and Astrology

Originally the sciences of astronomy and astrology were one; in fact the term *astrology*[14] etymologically describes this early science (and in fact our modern science of astronomy) better than the term now used for its current descendent. Only as astrology acquired its other meanings did the need for distinguishing between the original meaning of astrology (which astrologers designated as natural astrology) and those which it had gradually acquired through the ages (the latter group astrologers designated as juridical astrology[15]).

Although this twofold division of astrology is very

ancient, the original, primary meaning is far older.
The origins of natural astrology go back to man's
first appearance on earth. Immediately after his
creation, he became very interested not only in his
Creator but also in the works of his Creator. As the
book of Genesis teaches us, the first man named the
animals, was given the work of tending the garden
in which God had placed him, and given dominion
over all other created forms of life on this earth—the
entirety of which were the results of God's creative
activity. Beyond this his interest in the vaster areas
of God's activities soon arose; the presence of the
opening verses of Genesis bear witness to this fact.

The roots of the second division of astrology and
its acquired meanings are also very ancient.[16] They
go back to those events which are called *The Fall*.
After the first man had been expelled from his gar-
den-paradise, many of his descendents began to with-
draw more and more from worshipping the only true
God and Creator. Thus, although he ceased to give
the one God credit for having made all nature, he
nonetheless continued to have an intense interest in
it and to scrutinize it. Soon he recognized (or regained
the realization of) his dependence (as well as that
of all life) upon the sun for warmth and existence.

Because of the primacy of the sun's importance
for him, in time he deified it and began to worship
it. As he continued to watch it and the other heavenly
bodies, he began to note certain apparently self-
evident facts: Certain "stars" were fixed; others,
like the sun, moved in the heavens. He also noted
that the moon moved and that all these moving bodies
appeared to revolve around the earth as their center.
The sun rotated daily, the moon in a longer period
of time, and the moving stars in still longer. The
latter, which we call planets, appeared to him to have
not only their normal forward motion but also at

times to stand still and to have retrograde motion, i.e., they would at times cease their regular motion and then seemingly move in the reverse direction.

As these observations continued, man gradually associated certain coincidences in nature—many of which were and are purely accidental—with the motions of these moving stars. Probably next to the sun, man paid more attention to the moon, and, as a result of real apparent effects of the moon upon the earth, he also deified the moon. Similarly, deification spread to the planets,[17] and astronomy began to assume more and more a religious aspect, gradually becoming intricately, intimately, and inseparably associated with his polytheistic religion. In this manner natural astrology (astronomy) took its first step toward becoming astrobiology[18] and eventually juridical astrology.

Undoubtedly this deification of the heavenly bodies increased his interest in learning all he could concerning their movements and to be able, if possible, to predict their future behavior. To accomplish these goals, some sort of a calendar was needed. He also required one so that he could execute his religious responsibilities to his deities.

Another reason which prompted man to invent some means of recording the passage of time concerned a variety of needs[19] arising out of his cultivation of crops. These factors, and perhaps others, contributed to his gradual association of the movements of the heavenly bodies with the passage of time and, in particular, with his various manufactured calendars. In consequence he began to record the apparent motions of the mobile celestial bodies. The earliest known records of man's astronomical observations[20] come from the Mesopotamian Valley,[21] the very place to which historians and the Bible trace the origins of juridical astrology. These records appear to be more valuable and accurate for the motions of Venus and of the moon[22] than even for the motion of the sun.

From Religious Astronomy to Astrobiology

To facilitate the acquisition of the information man needed to satisfy the demands of his religion, of his agriculture, and of his budding scientific interest, he constructed all over the world large astronomico-religious sites, such as those huge megalithic places in Britain and the ziggurats of Mesopotamia. These structures, in addition to being used for purposes of worship, aided him in making astronomical observations, in marking solstices, and in noting the important calendrical aspects for agriculture. Because of the centrality of the religious elements, the natural astrologers (astronomers) became priests; they were what we might call astronomical priests or priestly astronomers. Although in a given person, either the scientific or the religious aspect was predominant, the two aspects became inseparably intertwined: thus the religious sites became the repositories of the accumulation of scientific data.[23]

At the beginning of this period and for some considerable time thereafter, the observations remained essentially scientific. Because these religious sites were the centers of, and in time became the sole or chief repositories of, all learning, the priests gradually recorded not only the scientific data, but also the myths which grew up around their pagan deities. As the original meaning and use of these myths were lost, these priests, and other men began to associate magical elements with the heavenly gods. In this way astrology, as the science of astronomy was then called, began to move in the direction of magic and divination.

Even now, the priestly scientists—as they would
for centuries, millennia—preferred to ascertain what
the fates and/or the gods intended to do in the future
by other means than astrology. This neglect of using
astrological divination would continue for eons of
time even after the astrological process had been
initiated. One favorite method, which continued to
have preference even after the birth of mundane astrology, was that of examining the entrails and other
parts of birds and animals, especially the liver. They
used this method because they assumed (1) that the
"soul" of the animal was primarily located in its
liver, and (2) that the deity who accepted the sacrifice identified himself with the animal or bird offered.
Therefore, as a consequence, men (3) assumed that
the animal's "soul" became fully identified with that
of the god, and (4) that the creature's liver reflected
and revealed the will and the mind of that god.[24]

Although these early stages in the development
of astrology appear to be more or less worldwide
in scope, both the recording of the astronomical data
(as noted earlier) and the origin of modern juridical
astrology appear to have begun in the Mesopotamian
Valley. There, in mighty Babylon, the seat of all the
ancient satanic powers, "a fantastic scheme of astrology was built up, and indeed, was regarded by
the Babylonians as the chief and most worthy object
of the underlying science." [25] How did this happen?
How could it occur? How was the barrier and the
border between science and magic crossed?

Undoubtedly a very important and real, although
probably subconscious and undoubtedly psychological, factor was the increase of power over their fel-
lowman that these scientist-priests had. Their knowledge of science, of religion, and of education give
them a unique position of power and influence in Mesopotamia. Through their endeavors astronomy-astrol-

ogy became "not merely the queen of the sciences. . . [but] mistress of the world." [26] In this manner they became the custodians or librarians of the world's scientific and other knowledge. At these temple libraries the data was recorded in cunneiform on clay tablets. The astronomical data may have spanned some three millennia or so. Thus some of the data that archaeology has uncovered may have originated in the antediluvian period.

Somewhere in the long, checkered career of Babylon, the next—really the first—major step in the conversion of natural astrology (astronomy) to juridical astrology occurred—the emergence of embryonic astrology or astrobiology. The time at which this happened and the name of the people who first took this giant step has been lost in antiquity. Nonetheless the general locale of the event is known— Babylon or Mesopotamia. Perhaps the inventors were the Sumerians,[27] as the great epic myth, *The Enuma Annul Elli*, suggests. But since this myth, at least to some extent, was reworked by the succeeding Semites and by the later inhabitants of the neo-Assyrian and neo-Babylonian empires, the originators of astrobiological aspects of this myth are unknown.

Nonetheless the steps in its emergence may be traced.[28] As stated previously, early man became intensely aware of the vast universe surrounding him —especially as he began to worship the sun, the moon, and eventually the other "wanderers" of the skies as his deities. Because of the resulting religious needs and because of agricultural needs, he designed an instrument to record the passage of time—that which we call the calendar. Originally he based his calendar upon various devices, none of which was entirely satisfactory.

As man remembered and began to record the passage of time and events, he began to recognize the relationship of the passage of time to the motions of the sun, moon, and planets[29]—in other words, to his gods. He also associated the alternation of light and darkness (day and night) and of the four periods (seasons) of the year with these heavenly, divine entities. He soon noticed that the year with its four seasons was related to the moon's behavior—namely, that there are about twelve lunar cycles for every single solar one. In Babylon, the astronomer-priests began to mark out their calendar (i.e., the progression of the year) by identifying each segment with the various "stars" which arose at that period.

Factors such as these fostered in the fertile imaginations of fallen man, especially when the satanically inspired idea developed that the heavenly events and the earthly ones were intimately inter-related. His earlier assumptions regarding divination from the entrails of creatures, and his conviction that the stars and his deities were either one or else very intimately connected, led him to assume a theory of the divine government of the world—one in which there was a one-to-one correspondence between the history of mankind and the astronomical phenomena exhibited by his "star"—god. For example, if the king of Ur were to fight and defeat the king of Sippur, this historical event signified that the god of Ur had fought and conquered the god of Sippur and that Ur's god now was the chief heavenly ruler (or prime minister) of the assembly of the gods.

Needless to say such a theory fostered even more the collection and recording of astronomical data, historical events, and divinational information—especially the interpretative elements whereby certain aspects of the liver and certain kinds of historical phenomena were associated. Moreover, it suggested that astronomical configurations and events would indicate the heavenly events even as the liver did the will and mind of the god to whom that animal was offered. Hence these astronomic priests began to collect and to associate the coincidental heavenly phenomena with the events of man's history. Gradually, as had been done with the earlier divinational material, interpretations of the astronomical phenomena developed.[30]

This accumulation and development of this interpretative astronomical data was enhanced by the use of the earlier divinational material, by recollection of "catastrophic heavenly events" corresponding to drastic historical events, and by the association of ideas (this procedure had also been used earlier in obtaining the divinational interpretative information) which often were only a mere pun[31]—a play on words.

In such a manner, astrobiology arose, based on man's many false assumptions. From this time onward until the Reformation, the concept, *astrology*, would have two distinct meanings: its original meaning, now to be designated as natural astrology, denoting the science of the stars; and its acquired meaning, a divinational, magical way for determining the will and mind of the gods as related to matters of public importance and to items which affected man's general welfare.

Astrobiology, or mundane astrology, was not concerned with the welfare of the individual. Even the preoccupation with the person of the king was not individually inspired. It resulted from the close connection of the king with that people's chief deity and primarily with his close relationship to the public welfare. The zenith of this form of early divinational astrology was reached in Babylon in the sixth century B.C.,[32] prior to its fall.

Sometime later, probably after Babylon had fallen

to the Medes and Persians, the next major step in
divinational astrology was taken. The ingredients had
been present for some time before an unknown Babylonian priest intuitively connected the lunar cycle and
the belief concerning the sun's passage during a year
through the ecliptic. The perfection of the ecliptic
and the creation of the zodiac do not seem to have
been accomplished until after the neo-Babylonian
empire had come to an end. Nonetheless, the intimate
association of these two ideas, and the association
with the twelve heavenly constellations into the concept of the zodiac, gave to mundane astrologers all
the necessary ingredients to take that one last step
toward fully developed juridical astrology—the prediction of the future for individuals and the casting
of horoscopes.

The Origins of Genethliacal Astrology

Long before the fall of Babylon to the Persians,
the Babylonian astronomico-priests were very familiar with the fixed stars, the sun, the moon, and the
planets as well as their relationship to the calendar
with its seasons. Thus the majority of the necessary
ingredients for casting a horoscope were available
for centuries prior to its invention. By the middle
of the Persian period, the zodiac[33] had been invented
by an unknown Babylonian priest and had been
divided into twelve equal sections of thirty degrees
each. In some manner or other a Babylonian priest
had intuitively associated the lunar cycle, the annual
course of the sun in the celestial ecliptic, and the
twelve constellations of stars which seemingly lie on
this ecliptic.

This priest (or a succession of priests) began to
perfect the zodiac; in time one of them began to
graphically represent the heavens and to invent and

name the twelve signs of the horoscope. No one knows
how the signs received the names which they share
in common with the twelve constellations of the celestial zodiac. The reason for the names given the constellations is likewise an enigma—of the twelve, only
Leo has any resemblance to its name. Moreover, the
exact configuration of stars have not remained con-
stant over the years, and some of them have fewer
stars than they had at one time.

Furthermore, astrologers make another stranger
(at least to twentieth century minds) association.
These twelve signs are divided into four groups of
three signs each—corresponding to the ancient belief
that fire, earth, air, and water constituted the four
elements. Thus astrologers speak of fiery, earthy,
airy, and watery signs. The origin of this classifica-
tion is likewise unknown.

Within the Persian (or, at the latest the early
Grecian) period, individual, birth horoscopes[34] were
invented, and the birth of genethliacal astrology occurred. During this period natural astrology (astronomy) tended to be crystalized and to be used only
(or almost only) for genethliacal purposes.

Why had genethliacal astrology not emerged
earlier? Why had mundane astrology not enjoyed
the popularity of other means of divination? Why
hadn't it and other divinational means been used
earlier than they were for purposes of disclosing the
future and other important information for individuals? All that can be said has already been indicated
above because: (1) other methods of revealing the
future were more popular and were considered to be
more accurate; (2) "the terrible Babylonian idea of
the Fate which rules alike stars and gods and men"[35]
had not yet been fully associated with the accumu-
lated astrological-astronomical data; and (3) until the
invention of the art of casting horoscopes had been

perfected, it was not possible to predict the future
except in a very general manner. Now it was possible
to give varying "detailed" predictions of future
events for different individuals even when their birth
differed in time or space by a relatively small amount.
Horoscopes of individuals, recorded in clay tablets,
have been found dating from the third century B.C.[36]

The one remaining aspect of the astrological zodiac, the thirty-six decans, constitutes the sole contribution of the Egyptians[37] to astrology. They made
far more contributions to the calendar, being responsible essentially for our present 365-1/4 day year.
Their calendar was called the Sothic calendar and
was introduced in 45 B.C. to Rome by Julius Caesar.
He made a modification in the length of certain
months and converted the Roman calendar into a
modified Sothic one. With the single change made
by Augustus, this Julian calendar remained intact
until about two centuries ago; then a slight change
converted it into the more accurate Gregorian calendar.

The Sothic calendar was divided into twelve
months, each month being composed of three decans.
These decans were related to the extension of the
earth's equator to the heavens; thus the decans were
properly divisions of the heavenly equator—not of the
heavenly ecliptic. They were not, then, really related
to the zodiac, the divisions of the heavenly ecliptic.
Since, however, "the extent in the latitude of decads
and zodiacal signs was not clearly stated, the star
groups and the star lore relative to them could easily
flow from one system to the other." [38] This flow actually took place and gradually the decans were
added to the zodiacal system.

This addition of the decans to the zodiac did not
occur before the Hellenistic period[39] and may have
been as late as the first or second century B.C.[40]

The decans, themselves, are much older and first appear on coffin lids of the Middle Kingdom; they divided the three hundred sixty day Egyptian year into thirty-six parts ("decans"). Each of these correspond to one-third of a zodiacal sign or ten degrees of the ecliptic. Only two of these decans can be identified positively with a celestial constellation or star.[41]

Genethliacal Astrology—From Its Birth To Its Zenith

Although Plato and the Greeks had heard of astrology, their knowledge of it was very limited until the third century B.C. Apparently the pre-Homeric astronomy was derived chiefly from Egypt, and these basic concepts were modified in the interval through the influence of the Greek "philosophical scientists" and by the gradual permeation of some Babylonian ideas. The infusion of the latter was accelerated by the conquests of Alexander, but, not until about 280 B.C. was effective knowledge of astrology brought to the Greeks by Berosus, a Chaldean priest.[42] Somewhat later, Attalus I of Pergamus,[43] invited another Chaldean, Soudines, to his court, c. 238 B.C. There Soudines practiced various forms of magic and divination, including astrology.

The Greeks, having borrowed astrology from Babylon, proceeded to appropriate it and to transform it. They did not, however, contribute any really new element to astrology; but what they did was to give it its present form and to prepare the tables which are still being used. The Stoics, a Greek philosophical school, synthesized the data from Babylon with their astronomy. Others, like Cleostratos of Tenedos, may have embellished astrology.[44] Certainly some Greek astrologers enlarged the scope of astrology until it was closely connected with almost all

the known sciences: botany, chemistry, zoology, min-
eralogy, anatomy, and medicine. During this period
all kinds of colors, metals, stones, plants, drugs,
and animals were associated with the planets and
placed under their influence. The zenith or climax
of these Grecian transformations was accomplished
by that great Alexandrian, Graeco-Roman-astrono-
mer-astrologer, Claudius Ptolemaeus. Modern astrology is based almost entirely upon his astronomi-
cal-astrological works.

Claudius Ptolemaeus is popularly called Ptolemy
and is chiefly known for his astronomical scheme
which endured until Galileo's time. His astrology was
essentially based upon Chaldean ideas and data
which were intermingled with some ancient Babylonian and Egyptian concepts interspersed with
Greek astronomical beliefs. Although he may not realize it, the twentieth century astrologer still uses
essentially the system and data synthesized and produced by the Ptolemaic school.

Astrology in our modern understanding, therefore,
arose out of polytheistic ideas and concepts. In all
periods of its comparatively brief life, it has been
closely associated with magic and divination. In fact
it is but one of many ways of claiming to divine the
future. Astrology may have derived from hepatoscopy,[45] as Morris Jastrow has suggested.

In the very early periods it was indistinguishable
from astronomy, and was not associated with pagan
worship and magic. It really did not exist with the
modern meaning before the end of the seventh century B.C., and probably not until the third century
B.C. In the latter century it began to develop rapidly, and between that century and the second century
A.D., the chief elements of astrology—the zodiac and
all its elements, the decans, the concept of individual

horoscopes—were fused into a homogeneous entity with the more ancient Mesopotamian data and ideas by the Greek genius, the final form being given to it by Ptolemy and his school. Thus astrology did not really, in a very meaningful sense, begin to burst forth into full blossom until a century or so after our Lord had brought the brilliant radiance and illumination of the true God into our world again.

NOTES

1. To use McLuhan's terminology.

2. From a recent McGraw-Hill publication; see Jonas, David and Klein, Doris: *Man-child.* The authors seek to establish that man is entering an age of his infantilization.

3. Astrologers talk about the influence or control of the stars, but they are using the term, *stars,* incorrectly. By it they are referring to most of the members of our solar system—only one of which is a star. By this term they mean the sun (the only true star of the group), the satellites of the sun (our planets), and the moon (the earth's satellite).

4. If its influence ever completely left the church—see chapter 3, pp. 79 ff.

5. Jude 3.

6. Many astrologers are very deterministic; they consider that the stars reveal the destiny of each individual. Others, perhaps the majority, believe (or at least pay lip service to the belief) that the stars only strongly influence the future; the individual himself may alter the influence of the stars.

7. The moon and the eight planets. All of these with the exception of Pluto (which is invisible to the naked eye) appear to move within the path of the heavenly zodiac, a path which extends about 8 degrees on either side of the celestial ecliptic.

8. See pp. 7, 8.

9. The sun, the moon, and the eight planets.

10. The Greek word from which horoscope is derived carries the meaning of watching that which is rising. Hence the horoscope originally was only concerned with the point

of the zodiac which appeared to be rising over the horizon at the exact moment of birth.

11. The description of the horoscope, its contents, and its interpretation is very brief and has been considerably simplified. The casting and the interpretation of a horoscope is much more complicated and requires the use of a number of "tools."

12. See, for example, the *Sunday Star-Ledger* for January 3, 1971.

13. Anonymous quotation; see *Eternity,* October, 1970, p. 10.

14. See pp. 7, 8. Astronomy is derived from the Greek word for star and for distribute, manage. Thus it properly deals only with a restricted area of the entire science that we call astronomy—i.e., the system of laws governing the stars.

15. Juridical astrology deals with the divinational aspects of astrology, including all those elements which go into current popular fads, whether these deal with individuals or groups of persons, e.g. nations.

16. According to T. K. Cheyne, *The Prophecies of Isaiah* (London: C. Kegan Paul & Co., 1880), I, 296, the earliest known "standard" astrological work dates from the sixteenth century B.C., and is written on seventy clay tablets

17. Symbols of Sin, the Moon-god, Shamesh, the Sungod, and Ishtar, the goddess of love, are found in stone carvings dating c. fourteenth century B.C. This deification of the planets (sun and moon, at least) is, of course, much older.

18. A term coined by Berthelot to denote the belief that the movement of the stars are related to all earthly phenomena, and that they control farming, husbandry, health, and the entire social order.

19. The need to know when to plant seed (in agriculture) was important, as was (were) the agricultural season(s). In Egypt, where the Nile overflows its banks each year, in order to avail themselves of the sole supply of water for crops, it was essential to know when this innundation would occur.

20. Various times have been assigned to the beginning of these various known records. The more conservative dates place their origin at two to four millennia before Christ.

21. The first recording of astronomical data appears to be Semetic in origin. No Sumerian or earlier records have been found yet.

22. The earliest astronomical tables, based on observation, appear to deal with movements of Venus (from the reign of Ammisaduqa, c. 1650 B.C.) and of the moon (probably from the time of Sargon I, c. 1850 B.C.)

23. See p. 20.

24. Clay and bronze tablets which were used in teaching divination by hepatoscopy have been uncovered by archaeology. These models of the animal's liver were divided along the edge into sixteen parts, each of which had the name of a deity and each of which corresponded to that division of the heavens where this particular god (dess) lived. The opposite side had a line which divided the liver into day and night. These models clearly show how the liver of the sacrificial animal was considered to be a micro image of the universe as a whole. It discloses how the god's mind or will is reflected in the liver, and how it is brought into intimate connection with the heavenly bodies—the initiation of the assembly of the gods acting in unison.

25. Dampier, W. C., *A History of Science* (Cambridge: The University Press, 1966), 3 ff.

26. *Ibid.*, p. 4.

27. No astrological omen texts or other astrological data which undisputably comes from the Summerians have been found. No astrological omen texts which date from the old Babylonian era have been found; there has been uncovered only one tablet with omens which could properly be called astrological and which may date from this or from the next era and locale. Yet astrological tablets outside Babylonia (Elam, Mari, Qatua, Boghazhoy, Nuzi, and one from Nippur from the middle Babylonian period) have been discovered. This evidence, coupled with those bits of information which pertain to Babylonia, indicates that astrobiology in some form or other existed in the old Babylonian era in Babylon.

28. Although not necessarily in the order stated.

29. See p. 20.

30. In fact, astrological divination appears to have arisen from hepatoscopy and always (at least in Mesopotamia) to have been associated intimately with it.

31. In fact a study of all omen texts reveals that, whether

they were hepatoscopic (divination by the liver) or astrological omens, only in exceptional cases is there any logical connection between the portent and the prediction.

32. Dampier, *loc. cit.*

33. Thus the zodiac may have been invented while Daniel was still living.

34. See, for example, McIntosh, Christopher, *The Astrologers and Their Creed* (New York: Praeger, 1969), pp. 8ff.

35. Dampier, *op. cit.*, p. 38.

36. The earliest known horoscope is dated c. 409 B.C. according to some authorities; e.g., Ganquelin, Michael, *The Cosmic Clocks* (New York: Avon Books, 1969), p. xix.

37. Astrology was not popular in Egypt until the sixth century B.C. Perhaps this accounts for their meager contribution to astrology.

38. Sarton, George, *A History of Science* (New York: Wiley & Sons, 1964), Science Editions, p. 119.

39. There is no evidence for the zodiac in Egypt prior to the Hellenistic period.

40. The earliest known Egyptian astrological records belong to the second century B.C.

41. Sirius and Orion.

42. At least traditionally speaking! Berosus is reported to have migrated to Cos (an island) where he established a school in which he taught the Babylonian knowledge recorded in cunneiform. The actual time of the origin of the astrological zodiac is unknown, but it did not occur prior to the Persian era—i.e., it originated some time between the third and sixth centuries before Christ.

43. Another traditional idea.

44. He probably recognized the constellations through which the sun, moon, and planets appear to move. He also may have divided those constellations among twelve equal parts of the celestial ecliptic. Thus he may be responsible for the close association of the astrological zodiacal signs and the constellations of the imaginary heavenly ecliptic.

45. The common designation for a planet is a compound ideograph ("word") whose two component elements signify a "dead Sheep." Thus when the planets began to be used as omens, the name of the "slain sheep" was applied to them even as "augery" (divination by means of the flight

of birds) was applied by the Romans to every kind of divination. See also p. 24, especially footnote 24, p. 33.

II

The Bible in the Astrologer's Den

Astrology, like every cult or sect, seeks to establish favorable connections with extant world religions by using one or more of three approaches:

1. Frequently the cult or sect will argue that its teachings and those of the competing world religions are compatible. For example, the Rosicrucians often maintain that no conflicts exist between their teachings and those of Christianity; in other words, they state that a person can be both a Christian and a Rosicrucian at the same time.

2. Another device is for the cult or sect to attempt to show that their teachings are identical with some (or all) of the doctrines of the competing world religions. For instance, many of the present-day cults and religions which teach reincarnation attempt to prove that the Christian (and Jewish) Scriptures also proclaim this tenet.

3. The third procedure which the cultist utilizes is to try to establish that his (i.e. his faith's) teachings are the real (but often secret) ones of his competitive world faith. An example of this is Christian Science; it claims that it reveals the real, Christian doctrine.

The modern astrological attempt to establish a rapport with the present-day world religions has met with varying success. In the non-Christian world, it has been far more successful than in the Judaeo-Christian worlds. The reason for this is at least two-fold: (1) Both astrology and the non-Christian religions either are polytheistic, pagan religions which agree on most, if not all, of the fundamental assumptions[1] they make or else are developments of original polytheism into atheistic,[2] humanistic, and/or pantheistic[3] religions, and (2) most of these pagan religions have used astrology (in some form or other) as a part of their religious beliefs and practices over the centuries. Thus, for them, astrology has always been more or less an integral part of the accepted, established order.

In the dealings of astrology with both Judaism and Christianity, the situation has been and is far different. Notwithstanding the claims of astrologers and their devotees, neither faith has ever accepted astrology universally and uniformly over the centuries.[4] There have been individual professing members of both faiths who have embraced astrology, but the general trend in each has been against practicing it. Consequently in most ages, astrologers and their devotees have been hard pressed to establish a meaningful rapport with either faith. They have been forced into making fantastic assertions and often have used fabrications in their diversified approaches to this problem. Only in the latter half of the present century, after the effects of destructive Biblical criticism and, frequently, the well-intentioned but equally disastrous effects of unintelligent orthodoxy, have seriously undermined the permanent, true values and teachings of Christianity (and of Judaism, to a lesser degree) in the eyes of the world (and often of their own followers), has astrology finally reached its hey-day. It has seemingly been able finally (momentarily, at least) to bridge in an effective manner the traditional rejection by the Judaeo-Christian faiths, and appears to be accepted almost universally, while its opponents seem to be crying against a strong wind.

A few of the fabulous, hyperbolic arguments advanced by astrology in making this current rapport with Judaism and Christianity are: (1) the assertion that Joseph, Abraham, Isaiah, Moses, David, as well as many of the other Biblical prophets, were practicing astrologers; (2) the insistence that the Bible is filled with astrological symbolism which has never been understood or interpreted correctly by either Christianity or by science. The reason, astrologers say, is obvious; neither the church nor science understands or accepts astrology. Perhaps the most interesting examples they cite are the first and the last chapters of the Bible. According to them, the first chapter of Genesis is an incomplete description of the zodiac, and the last chapter of the book of Revelation is filled with, as yet, uninterpreted astrological symbolism; (3) the appeal to the writings of border-line and of rejected Jewish or Christian sects; and (4) the use of absolute fabrications, such as the claim that the Christians inaugerated the concept of the world being flat or that astronomy only came into existence after 500 A.D. as a Christian effort to conform to the dictates of the Christian Church. [5]

Two of the more interesting attempts of the nineteenth century (which contributed, psychologically, at least to the present astrological boom) are *Mazzaroth*[6] by Frances Rolleston (1862) and *Astrology of the Old Testament*[7] by Karl Anderson (1892). The first author asserted that "the promises and prophecies revealed to Adam, Seth, and Enoch" are expressed by astral names and emblems. She also claimed fairly exact equations to exist between the Scriptures and the stars. She, like many other astrological cultists, found the chief revelations of the last book of the Bible to be zodiacal. Anderson also presupposed a similar cosmology to hers, and he linked the twelve signs of the zodiac to the twelve tribes of Israel. Interestingly, he found that *angel* was a corruption of *angle* and that Jesus, when stooping and writing in the ground, was actually casting a horoscope!

The scriptural references to which the astrologers seem to appeal most frequently are: the first chapter of Genesis (especially verses 14 f.); Numbers 24:17; Judges 5:20, Amos 5:8; Matthew 2:1-13 (the Star of Bethlehem); and the Book of Revelation. Let us now turn to the Scriptures and see if these fabulous claims of astrology are valid.

Were the Patriarchs and the Prophets Astrologers?

Nowhere in the sacred writings of the Jews or of the Christians does there exist the slightest evidence that any one of the patriarchs or the prophets were familiar with the methods of divination by means of the stars—much less that anyone was a practicing astrologer. The best evidence for this is found in the Scriptures themselves. Concerning Abraham,[8] one should read Genesis 12:1-9, 13:1-14; 14-18; 14:8-15, 21, 17:1-33 and 22:1-19; and concerning Joseph,[9] Genesis 37:1-36, 40:1-45 and 49:1-32.

An unbiased reading of these selections (or of the entirety of the scriptural passages) made by any person without preconceived motions reveals absolutely no evidence whatsoever to suggest that Abraham, Isaac, Jacob,[10] or Joseph possessed any knowledge of astrology, much less that any practiced it. On the contrary, the Bible stresses the dependence of the patriarchs upon God for all things and that God alone revealed to them the extraordinary information which they had. In the case of Joseph, there are two passages which astrologers (and cultists) have used to suggest that he was an astrologer. These are Genesis 37:9[11] and Genesis 41:45. In addition they assert that the prophetic song of Jacob[12] (Gen-

esis 49:1-32) also has references to the astrological
zodiac. Two of these will be considered later, but the
third, Genesis 41:45, has only two possible astrological references: Joseph's new name which signifies
"the one to whom secrets are revealed," and his marriage to a daughter of a priest of On (Heliopolis).
His new name is a natural one; he has just revealed
to Pharaoh the meaning of his dream. Genesis em-
phasizes the fact that Joseph received his information
from God—NOT from the STARS! Likewise in his
marriage to this priest's daughter, there is nothing
to suggest that he received any special instruction
in magic or in divination. Moreover, as shown earlier,[13] astrology did not really take hold in Egypt
until much later—the sixth century B.C.—and was
not fully embraced by the Egyptians until the Hellenistic period. Therefore very little exists, if any at
all, to suggest that Joseph or that any Egyptian used
an embryonic form of astrology, like astrobiology.

Astrological claims for Moses,[14] Balaam,[15]
Isaiah,[16] David,[17] and Daniel[18] have also been
set forth. Like the patriarchs, the prophets[19] may
behave in an unusual manner (e.g. Isaiah[20] and
Ezekiel[21]), may have unusual experiences, and
may know matters which even the most knowledge-
able or wisest man does not know. Yet there does
not exist the slightest hint or suggestion that any one
of them ever practiced astrology or any other kind
of divination. Even Moses who had been given all
the wisdom of Egypt and who may have known their
divinational methods and their arts of magic, was
able to perform his miracles only, as the Scriptures
so clearly point out, because of God. He was God's
agent, and he lived very close to Him. In all of this
he was a typical Hebrew prophet.

Even in the case of Balaam, a heathen outsider,
there is no support whatever that he was familiar

with astrology and its practice. The fact that his home was in Mesopotamia, along the Euphrates River valley, only indicates the POSSIBILITY that he may have been aware of the existence of some form of embryonic astrology, perhaps astrobiology. It does not suggest that he was an astrologer. Likewise, the prophecy that he makes concerning a star (Num. 24:17) has reference to a person, the Messiah, who will be a descendent of Jacob; it can have no reference to the Star of Bethlehem or to any astrological phenomenon. The Scriptures themselves continually stress Balaam's inability to perform that for which he was hired—to condemn Israel. On the contrary, they insist that Balaam derived all his powers from the one true God and that he could only reveal what God had told him.

When we come to Daniel, it is here alone that there exists perhaps the greatest amount of scriptural evidence for the possibility of his being an astrologer. Nonetheless, even for Daniel, a scrutiny reveals the following facts very clearly: (1) Daniel was trained in the wisdom of the Babylonians; this instruction may have included the arts of Babylonian magic and divinations, including their developing astrology. (2) He is included in the group of wise men who were to be killed if Nebuchadnezzar was not told the contents of his dream and then its interpretation (chapter two). And (3) yet he is in some ways always distinct from the other members of this group of wise men and divinators. Moreover (4) the Biblical terms used in Isaiah 49:13 and in Daniel 2:27 (cf. also 3:27) are not used to designate Daniel, although they refer to Babylonian masters of the art of astrology and other forms of divination. On the contrary, the Biblical account everywhere stresses the fact that Daniel, like the other prophets and patriarchs, owed his position of superiority in knowledge, wisdom,

and understanding to his God to whom he was ever
loyal and true.

The only evidence of astrological influence and
ideas in Judaism is very late.[22] It obviously was
not directly introduced, but only permeated Jewish
thinking through the means of syncretic Hellenism,
gradually gaining an ever-widening acceptance. The
usual practice of Judaism was to attribute the origin
of astrology to the fallen angels (e.g. Enoch 8:3).
Only in the post-Christian, oral traditions recorded
in the Talmud[23] may be found the origins of the
suggestion that Abraham had been an astrologer,
e.g., Abraham is stated to have worn a large astrological tablet in which the fate of all men could be
read. In it Abraham saw that he would have no sons
after Isaac, but God told him:

> Away with your astrology; for Israel there is no
> planet.—Shab. 156a.

This is not an isolated example. Elsewhere Abraham is associated with astrologers, for example:

> A man to whom a son was born was met by an
> astrologer who, on seeing the child, declared that he
> was destined to become a bandit-chief (ἀρχιληστής)
> and must be put out in the desert. The father of the
> child refused until the astrologer's father told him
> to do just as his son had ordered. The father of the
> astrologer is God; the astrologer is Sarah; the child
> is Ishmael; and the father of the child is Abraham.
> —Deut. R IV 5 which refers to Gen. 21:10-12.

Much of the Talmudic writings, however, declare
that Abraham was not an astrologer. The evidence
of the Talmud is therefore not conclusive. It represents a transitional period in which astrology was
growing in popularity and influence in Judaism.[24]
It was only in the Middle Ages that astrology was
widely practiced and endorsed by the Jewish
people.[25]

Does the Bible Support (or Even Tolerate) Astrology and Astrologers?

The question can be simply, easily, and accurately answered in a single word—NO! Absolutely NO scriptural passage supports astrology, although several indicate awareness of its existence and that of the accompanying astral worship. Moreover, not a single reference even indicates tolerance of this art. There are a few places where it is condemned, either specifically or as a part of a more comprehensive disapproval. Consideration will first be made of the more prominent (or more frequently cited) Biblical verses used by astrologers to support their claims. No attempt will be made to refute the preposterous, unfounded claim made by many modern astrological cultist that the Book of Revelation is in reality an astrological textbook.[26] In conclusion, a few references will be noted where astrology is condemned outright.

The First Chapter of Genesis

In the beginning God created the heavens and the earth. The earth was formless and empty, and darkness lay upon the face of the deep, and the Spirit of God was moving over the surface of the waters.

God said: Let there be light, and there was light. God saw that the light was good and God divided the light from the darkness. The light God called Day and the darkness He called Night. There was evening and there was morning, one day.

God said: Let there be a firmament between the waters to divide waters from waters; so God made the firmament and separated the waters under the firmament from the waters above the firmament; and it was so. God called the firmament Heaven. There was evening and there was morning, a second day.

God said: Let the waters under heaven be

gathered into one place and let the dry land appear; and it was so. God called the dry land Earth and the gathering of the waters He called Seas, and God saw that it was good.

God said: Let the earth produce vegetation, various kinds of seed-bearing herbs and fruit-bearing trees with their respective seeds in the fruit upon the earth; and it was so. The earth produced vegetation, various kinds of seed-bearing herbs and fruit-bearing trees with their respective seeds in the fruit, and God saw that it was good. There was evening and there was morning, a third day.

God said: Let there be lights in the firmament of heaven to divide the day from the night; let them be for markers of seasons, days and years, and for luminaries in the firmament of heaven to shed light upon the earth; and it was so. God made the two great luminaries, the greater light for ruling the day and the lesser light with the stars for ruling the night. God set them in heaven's firmament to shed light upon the earth, to rule during the day and at night and to divide the light from the darkness; and God saw that is was good. There was evening and there was morning, a fourth day.

God said: Let the waters teem with shoals of living creatures and let birds fly above the earth along heaven's firmament. God also created the large sea-monsters, and all living, moving creatures with which the waters swarm according to their kind and every kind of winged bird. God saw that it was good and God blessed them; He said: Be fruitful, multiply and fill the waters in the seas and let birds multiply on earth. There was evening and there was morning, a fifth day.

God said: Let the earth bring forth living creatures after their kind, livestock, reptiles and wild beasts after their kind; and it was so. God made every kind of wild beasts and every kind of livestock and every kind of creeping things; and God saw that it was good.

Then God said: Let Us make man in Our image, after Our likeness, and let them bear rule over the fish in the sea, over the birds of the air, over the animals; over the whole earth and over all creeping things that crawl on the earth. So God created man in His image; in the image of God He created him; male and female He created them. God blessed them; God said to them: Be fruitful; multiply; fill the earth and subdue it; bear rule over the fish of the sea; over the birds of the air and over every living, moving creature on earth.

God further said: Behold, I have given you every seed-bearing plant over all the earth, and every fruit-tree, the fruit of which grows seed; it will be your food. And to all the animals on earth, to all the birds of the air and to every living creature that creeps on the earth I have given the green vegetation for food; and it was so. God saw that everything He had made was excellent, indeed. There was evening and there was morning, the sixth day.

Thus the heavens and the earth and all their host were completed. On the seventh day God ended His work which He had been doing. He rested on the seventh day from all the works He had accomplished. God also blessed the seventh day and consecrated it; because in it He rested from all His works, which in creating, He had formed.

These are the generations of the heavens and the earth in their creation.

Frequently the astrological cultist has claimed that this chapter incompletely describes the zodiac. Anyone who reads the above chapter, whether in an English translation or in the original Hebrew, can find no justification whatsoever for this claim; the only person who finds any hints of astrology are those who bring with themselves a predisposition to find such evidence. In fact, it is extremely difficult to discover any possible allusions to astrology. Only in their later writings do the Jews associate the zodiac with creation; for example:

The constellations [of the Zodiac] represent Creation: Aries is light and Taurus is darkness; Gemini represent the two sexes; Cancer symbolized man, who first retreats to nooks and corners like the

Crab, but eventually becomes brave as a Lion
(='Leo'); Virgo is a symbol of marriage; Libra
weighs all the deeds of man who, if found guilty, is
punished by Scorpio, a symbol of Gehinnon; after
purification in Mercy, however, he cast forth as
quickly as an arrow from a bow, represented by
Sagittarius, and becomes as innocent as a kid and is
purified by water poured by Aquarius (Pesik. R.20
[ed. Friedmann, p. 97b]).[27]

Outside of these late Jewish ideas which connected
Creation with the constellation of the zodiac, no evidence whatsoever exists for linking the first chapter
of Genesis to the astrological zodiac. The only possible exception lies in the word *markers* (verse 14);
this word may be construed to allude to astrological phenomena. It is embedded in a section dealing
with God's creation of the heavenly bodies: the sun,
moon, and stars. The passage goes on to state that
these bodies, especially those of the sun and of the
moon, are to be used for markers, for seasons, and for
days and years. The normal, common meanings of
the Hebrew word for markers agrees with the Berke-
ley translation cited above—namely, that the seasons and the days and years define or clearly identify
the meaning of the term, markers.

Yet the possibility remains, as some commentators have suggested, that the term, markers, is not
used with its ordinary meaning but that it indicates
here astrological events and portents, such as
eclipses, comets, constellations, meteors, weather-
indicators, the four quarters of the skies, and the
like. Outside of the fact that the word does not normally mean any of these, the chief difficulty lies in
trying to conceive how the sun and the moon could
be used with most of these significances. Moreover,
this view tends to overlook what Genesis is saying—
namely, that God made these heavenly bodies and
that they are to be used by man in this context

to aid him in constructing a calendar, or observing the proper seasons, and of seeing God's handiwork in the markers of the skies.

Also I will put enmity between you and the woman; also between your offspring and her offspring; He will crush your head and you will crush his heel. —Genesis 3:15

I will set My bow in the clouds; it shall be for a token of a covenant between Me and the earth.—Genesis 9:13

The men of Babylon made Succothbenoth, the men of Cuth made Nergal, the men of Hamath made Ashima.—II Kings 17:30

He deposed the priests whom the kings of Judah had appointed to burn incense at the high places in the cities of Judah and around Jerusalem, and those who burned incense to Baal, to the sun, to the moon, to the signs of Zodiac, and to all the host of heaven. —II Kings 23:5

Let those curse it who curse the day, who are skilled in rousing up Leviathan.—Job 3:8

By His power the sea is stilled, and by His understanding He smited through proud Rahab. By His breath the skies are cleared; His hand pierces the rushing serpent.—Job 26:12, 13

Can you bind the bonds of the Pleiades or loosen the girdle of Orion? Do you lead forth the signs of the zodiac in their season, or guide the Bear with her cubs?—Job 38:31-32

For the stars of heaven and its constellations shall not give their light; the sun shall be dark at its rising and the moon shall not send out its light.—Isaiah 13:10

How you are fallen from heaven, shining gleam, son of the morning! Chopped down to the ground, conqueror of nations!—Isaiah 14:12

In that day the Lord, with His relentless, great, and strong sword shall visit Leviathan, the fugitive snake, Leviathan, the coiling serpent, and shall slay the dragon which is in the sea.—Isaiah 27:1

Bel is bowed down, Nebo is stooping, their images are consigned to animals and to cattle; these which

are carried about are heavily loaded, making a bur-
den for the weary beast.—Isaiah 46:1

I will destine you for the sword, and you all shall
bow down to the slaughter; because when I called,
you did not answer, and when I spoke you did not
obey, but you did what was evil in My eyes and you
chose what displeased Me.—Isaiah 65:12

(Seek Him) who makes the Pleiades and Orion,
who turns blackness to morning and darkens day to
night; Him who calls the waters of the sea and pours
them out on the face of the earth—the Lord is His
name.—Amos 5:8

But you did carry Siccuth your king, and Kiyyun
the images, the star of your gods which you made for
yourselves. Therefore I will cause you to go into
captivity beyond Damascus, says the Lord; the God
of hosts is His name.—Amos 5:26, 27

Outside the Book of Revelation, the Star of Bethlehem (Matthew 2:1-12), and a few scattered references in Acts and the Pauline epistles, almost all
the potential astronomical and astrological passages
are found in the Old Testament. The passages quoted
above constitute the majority of the pertinent possible allusions, the most crucial ones except for the
places where eclipses[28] and meteor(ite)s[29] might
be mentioned and where the general information re-
lating to the stars[30] and condemnation of their
worship[31] occur.

One of the most interesting potential astronomi-
cal-astrological verses is the famous Messianic passage in Genesis 3:15. A very few brave scholars and
commentators, like Maunder, have suggested that it
refers to the constellations of Scorpio, Ophiuchus, and
Serpens. In these star groups the ancients saw a man
who was tramping a scorpion on its head with one
foot, who was strangling a snake, and who was
simultaneously bitten by the scorpion in the heel of
his other foot.

Needless to say, this picture of the celestial skies

and the contents of this verse bear striking resemblance to one another. But even if this verse does
allude to this heavenly spectacle, there does not exist
any astrological connotation in it. The Scriptures
here, as everywhere else, have been purged of all
pagan, polytheistic, pantheistic, and magical meanings. They *may* use mythological, pagan metaphors,
but, if they do, they are used either unconsciously
and are without significance, or they are deliberately
used as a weapon against these false pagan concepts.

Other Biblical terms or phrases which may refer
to astronomical phenomena, but which have absolutely *NO* astrological allusions are: the bow in the
Noahaic covenant (Genesis 9:13); the rushing serpent, the fugitive snake, or Leviathan (Job 3:8; 26:12
f.; Isaiah 27:1); Venus (Isaiah 14:12; 65:12); Jupiter
(Isaiah 65:12); Mars (II Kings 17:20); Saturn (Isaiah
26:1; Amos 5:26); and the Pleiades (Job 9:9; 38:31;
Amos 5:8) and Orion (*loc. cit.*; Isaiah 13:10). Many
of these passages contain Hebrew words whose meanings are very uncertain; consequently, even when
a reference to astronomical phenomena is certain,
it is by no means clear as to which phenomenon the
allusion is being made.

Ramm considers the most obvious reference in
the Bible to a constellation to be found in Job 26:13—
the celestial Dragon. Maunder and some other
scholars agree with this interpretation; many do not.
Likewise, Maunder and a few others find a similar
allusion in Job 3:8 and Isaiah 27:1. The contexts of
the two passages in Job permit this interpretaton,
although others are possible, but the context of Isaiah
27:1 is extremely unfavorable to it. The references
to the Pleiades are much more probable; almost
every commentator finds them to be mentioned in
Job 9:9, 38:31 and Amos 5:8. But they do not agree
as to which Hebrew word should so be translated.

Some suggest that all three terms of Job 9:9 refer
to portions of the Pleiades. Likewise, most of these
also find a mention of Orion in these three verses
and in Isaiah 13:10. The term *Kesil,* which is often
translated as Orion, may indicate a rebellious person.
Thus for the Hebrews, some Mesopotamian hero may
be viewed as a Titan rebel. To ask to loose the bands
of Orion "would be the same as asking, 'Canst Thou
bring down out of their places the stars that make
up this figure, and so, as it were, set the Titan
free?' " [32]

The claim that the Scriptures mention Venus,
Mars, Jupiter, and Saturn is very dubious. In Isaiah
14:12, the phrase, "the shining one," often has been
translated by the word *Lucifer.* Many scholars, however, believe that it should be translated as *Venus;*
this view is supported by the accompanying phrase,
"son of the morning." The other possible reference
to Venus contains one to Jupiter. These terms, often
translated as *Destiny* and *Fortune* (Isaiah 65:11), respectively, are uncertain as to their meaning. To establish the fact that they allude to Venus and Jupiter,
the terms must first be positively identified as two
Mesopotamian deities. Secondly, these specific
deities must be shown, respectively, to be the astral
deities of Venus and Jupiter. Scholars have been unable to meet both these requirements completely.
Similarly many expositors find a reference to Nergal
(a deity often connected with Mars) in 2 Kings 17:30
and to Nebo (an Assyrian deity which is identified
with Mercury) in Isaiah 26:1. The terms, *Siccuth* and
Kiyyun, of Amos 5:26 may be Mesopotamian deities
which are associated with Saturn.

The bow of Genesis 9:13 is the rainbow of the
clouds. With this, almost everyone except astrologers
agree. The bow in Scriptures always indicates a
weapon and in this verse reflects the ancient Biblical

(and non-Biblical) idea that the lightnings are the arrows of God (see, for example, Psalms 7:3; 18:14; Hab. 3:11) and are shot from God's bow (e.g. Psalm 7:12, Hab. 3:9). A very few scholars have hinted that Sagittarius may be the permanent memorial of God's covenant with Noah instead of the rainbow. There exists no real basis for this suggestion in the Scriptures themselves, and, even if it were true, the allusion has been stripped of all pagan concepts.

The following conclusions can be made with regard to these passages: (1) Genesis 9:13 has reference to the bow in the clouds, not to the bow in the stars. (2) Many of these passages are not using astronomical terms or figures of speech, but are making other literary, possibly mythological, allusions. (3) Some may mention certain astral deities and thus indirectly use either astral-religious or astronomical terms. (4) Some do refer to heavenly bodies. The latter, when they occur, are astronomical, not astrological, terms. They emphasize the fact that God made and controls everything in the universe. Therefore, they are saying: *Worship the True God!* NOT THE STARS!

More fruitful for astrological enthusiasts are Joseph's dream (Genesis 37:9-11) and the blessing of Jacob (Genesis 49:3-27). The eleven stars of Joseph's dream (the twelfth representing Joseph himself) and the twelve sons of Jacob are identified with the twelve constellations of the celestial zodiac and with the twelve zodiacal signs of the later horoscopes. Let us examine these passages:

> He had still another dream which he recounted to his brothers. "See here," he said, "I have had another dream. Take notice: The sun, the moon and eleven stars were bowing down to me." When he related this to his father and to his brothers, his father rebuked him; he said to him, "What sort of dream is this you had? Are we, your mother and I and your

brothers actually going to come, prostrating ourselves to the earth for you?" His brothers then felt
resentful toward him; but his father pondered the
words.

While Joseph's dream does refer to the sun, moon,
and eleven stars, there is no indication whatsoever
that these have any astrological (or even astronomical) meaning. In fact, his family is quick to identify
the sun and moon as referring to his parents, and
the eleven stars to his brothers.[33] Even Maunder
is quick to point out difficulties in finding any hints
of astrology or astronomy here. Certainly the astrologers and their devotees are straining at a gnat
and swallowing a camel to find any basis for allusions
to their faith here.

"Reuben, you are my first-born, my strength and
the first issue of my vitality; excellent in dignity,
prominent in prowess. Boiling over like water, you
will not retain pre-eminence; for you climbed up to
your's father's bed; you defiled my couch with your
climbing.

"Simeon and Levi are brothers; their weapons are
implements of violence. My soul, do not share in
their plot; my spirit, do not join their meeting; for
in their anger they murdered men and in their in-
solence they hamstrung oxen. A curse on their
anger, for it is fierce and on their rage, for it is
cruel. I will desperse them among Jacob and scatter
them in Israel.

"Judah, you are the one your brothers will praise;
your grip will be on the necks of your foes. May your
father's sons bow down to you. Judah, a lion's cub!
From prey you have gone high, my son! Like a lion
he stoops, he crouches; like an old lion; who would
rouse him? The scepter shall not depart from Judah, nor the leader's staff from between his feet until
Shiloh comes and Him the peoples shall obey. Hitch-
ing his foal to the vine, the donkey's foal to the
choice vine, he washes his clothes in wine, his gar-
ments in the juice of the grapes. His eyes are red
with wine and his teeth white with milk.

"Zebulun shall dwell by the seashore; he shall be a harbor for ships, with his flank toward Zidon.

"Issachar is a big-boned donkey, lying down between the sheep folds. When he finds rest enjoyable and the land pleasant, he bends his shoulder to carry loads and submits to servitude.

"Dan will judge his people as one of Israel's tribes. Let Dan be a serpent on the road, a horned snake in the path, that snips the horses' heels so that the rider falls backward. I am waiting, O Lord, for Thy salvation!

"Gad, raiders will assail him, but he assails their rear.

"From Asher, his food will be rich and he shall deliver royal dainties.

"Naphtali, a deer let loose; he produces beautiful sayings.

"Joseph is a fruitful bough, a fruitful bough by a spring, whose branches run over the wall. The archers sorely harassed him and shot at him; they have hated him; but his bow remains steady; his arms and his hands are reinforced by the aid of the Mighty One of Jacob, from the Shepherd, the Rock of Israel; through the God of your father, who will help you; through the Almighty who will bless you with blessings from heaven above; blessings from the deep that lies below; blessings of breasts and wombs. Your father's blessings surpass the blessings of my forebears, reaching what is choicest on the everlasting hills. They shall be on the head of Joseph, on the crown of him who was distinguished from his brothers.

"Benjamin, a tearing wolf; in the morning he devours prey, in the evening he divides loot."

The situation is somewhat different here. These verses do use certain metaphors, similes, and other figures of speech which may allow an astronomical identification, but definitely not the more fancied claims of some astrologers. A good example of the latter is Lyman E. Stowe.[34] He unequivocally says that Jacob really is stating the astrological fantasy of the purported influence of the twelve signs of the zodiac. He asserts that Reuben is Libra; Simeon,

Scorpio; Levi, Sagittarius; Judah, Capricornus; Dan, Aquarius; Naphtali, Pisces; Gad, Aries; Ashar, Taurus; Issachar, Gemini; Zebulun, Cancer; Joseph, Leo; and Benjamin, Virgo. Others by equally ingenious means identify Joseph, Dan, Reuben, and Judah with Taurus, Scorpio, Aquarius, and Leo, respectively. These argue that Jacob (in referring to Simeon and Levi) mentions that they killed men and hamstrung oxen. The oxen signify Joseph. In support they cite the Jerusalem Targum which interprets the verse as a reference to Joseph under the guise of an ox. The comparison of Joseph to a bull by Moses agrees with this identification. Jacob also compares Dan to a snake, Reuben to overflowing like water, and Judah to a lion's cub.

The rabbinic tradition is a better source for astrological connections. They connect Judah with the figure of a lion (Leo), Reuben to the likeness of a man or of a man's head (Aquarius), Ephraim to an ox [35] (Taurus), and Dan to an eagle. Even better still are the standards of the tribes—although these differ in their zodiacal associations. On the east were the standards of Judah, Issachar, and Zebulen (opposite Aries, Taurus, and Gemini); on the south, those of Reuben, Simeon, and Gad (opposite to Cancer, Leo, and Virgo); on the west, Ephraim, Manasseh, and Benjamin (opposite Libra, Scorpio, and Sagittarius); and in the north, Dan, Asher, and Naphthali (opposite Capricorn, Aquarius, and Pisces).

Some difficulties are to be encountered; for instance, Judah is not the only son of Jacob and/or tribe of Israel to be associated with a lion. Moreover astrologers do not agree which constellation corresponds to which son. Likewise the tribal standards, if they are taken as a basis for making comparisons to the zodiac, do not associate Judah with the con-

stellation of Leo. The question, therefore, arises
naturally: if the tribal standards and if the blessings
of Jacob are to be associated with the signs of the
zodiac, which association is correct? Examination
of the passage in the Bible does not suggest any
astrological allusions to the unbiased reader.

II Kings 23:5; Job 38:32

These two verses are the most crucial so far considered; the English word, *zodiac*, which is found in
both, is a translation of two different Hebrew words.
These words, however, are very similar in spelling
and in sound, differing only by the change of the L
in one to an R. The word found in II Kings 23:5 definitely means zodiac or planets, especially, as the stars
of good and bad fortune, in Rabbinic and later Hebrew; the crux of the matter is: what did it mean
in Biblical Hebrew? The cognate languages are not
particularly helpful; they do indicate a somewhat different meaning and a closer connection with the
ancient Sumerian mythologies. In Arabic, the word
signifies the twenty-eight mansions of the moon, and
in Assyrian, the mansions of the gods, i.e., the ter-
ritory assigned to them in the heavens. Even if the
correct meaning is *zodiac*, it does not mean the signs
of the *zodiacal* horoscope, but rather the twelve constellations of the heavenly zodiac. Above all, the context in which it occurs is the reformation introduced
by Josiah in which he removed the priests partici-
pating in the alien astral worship. Consequently it
has some astro-connotations. The author of Kings is
clearly saying: DO NOT WORSHIP THESE FALSE
STAR-GODS! WORSHIP THE ONE, TRUE,
CREATOR GOD!

In Job 38:32 several versions and commentators
translate the other word with the same meaning,
zodiac, yet they are probably wrong. The context de-

mands a non-astrological understanding; God is
speaking to Job. He begins by referring to the creation of the earth and by using a series of questions,
calling attention that He Himself is the Person who
made the universe and keeps it in order. It is against
this setting that God proceeds to ask Job this question. The answer is obvious: no man, not even Job,
can perform these tasks! Only God can do them.

Therefore these verses, although they may refer
to planets or to the twelve constellations of the celestial zodiac, are definitely conveying a message
which is the direct opposite of astrology—religious
or secular!

Judges 5:20-21

From heaven the stars fought; in their courses
they fought against Sisera. The brook Kishon swept
them away, that ancient brook, the brook Kishon.
March on, my soul, with strength!

The song of Deborah contains the one possible
example (Judges 5:20 f.) of a passage in the Old and
New Testaments which may not oppose astrology and
may indicate a tolerant (*not approving*) attitude
toward it. Astrologers claim that no shadow of doubt
exists that this passage is astrological. Moreover,
they assert that there is not and never has been a
river Kishon. To make such bold statements they
overlook several facts:

(1) The Kishon is not called a river; the word
Wadi, a brook, is a better translation. (2) Although
the verse seems to imply that the heavenly bodies
fought on the side of Israel and against Sisera, the
meaning is definitely not astrological. If it does mean
this, the allusion would either be to its religious aspects, that the planets were deities (i.e. the astro-
biological aspect), or to an idea found at times in
both Judaism and Christianity, which closely associated the heavenly bodies and the angels.[36]

The important fact, however, irrespective of those possible allusions, is the conviction and certainty so well expressed here that the God of Israel, the only true God, supported Israel in her battle against Sisera by employing all the forces of nature and all the animate beings He created to assist here in this struggle. Hence there is absolutely no suggestion that these stars exerted any influence or control, like that assumed by astrologers. Likewise, there exists no need to assume that there is an allusion to the pagan idea that the planets were animated beings which should be worshipped.

Again, the fact that this section is poetry must be remembered; greater freedom of expression exists in poetry than in prose. Thus, even if the poet, under the inspiration of God's Holy Spirit, is using an allusion to the ancient mythological, astro-biological ideas, he is stating that even the pagan forces are under the control of the God of Israel and can do nothing apart from Him. Thus again there exists no meaningful astrological allusion or support here.

The Star of Bethlehem (Matthew 2:1-12)

After Jesus had been born at Bethlehem in Judea during the reign of King Herod, there arrived wise men at Jerusalem from the east, inquiring, "Where is the newborn king of the Jews? For we saw his star in the east and we have come to worship him."

On hearing this, King Herod felt disturbed and with him all Jerusalem, so he called together all the chief priests and scribes of the people and demanded of them where the Christ should be born. They told him, "In Bethlehem of Judea, for so it is written by the prophet, 'And you, Bethlehem in the land of Judah, are by no means insignificant among Judah's rulers, for out of you a leader shall arise who will shepherd My people Israel.' "

Herod then summoned the wise men for a private interview and ascertained from them just when the star appeared. As he sent them to Bethlehem he said, "Go and find out every particular about the child and when you have learned this, report to me so that I too may go and do him honor."

After listening to the king they traveled on and, lo, the star they had seen in the east preceded them until it came and rested above the Baby's whereabouts. And on observing the star their joy was boundless.

Entering the house they saw the little One with His mother Mary and prostrating themselves they did Him homage. Opening their caskets they offered Him presents: gold, frankincense and myrrh. Then, due to divine warning in a dream not to return to Herod they went back to their own country by a different route.

The Star of Bethlehem is a favorite target of the cultists, especially those devoted to astrology. The latter frequently claim, without the slightest shred of evidence, that the star has been very embarrassing to Christianity because "its presence in Scripture is true astrology." This assertion is probably the most pretentious statement ever perpetrated by man. The Matthean passage has never been embarrassing to any real Christian; on the contrary, it has been one of the most cherished events in history—cherished in part because that star heralded the birth of the Saviour of mankind. Moreover, this passage mentions the star only four times, and it is definitely not astrological. On the other hand, the star undoubtedly was an astronomical phenomenon.

Let us note certain features concerning this unusual star.

1. The star had been visible over a considerable period of time; it also had been visible over a considerable expanse of the ancient world. The evidence for this is: (1) The visitors were Magi (see below). (2) The journey would take some time, even if the Magi had left immediately upon first seeing the star and even if their home was in a near-by country.

And (3) Herod killed all the children two years of age and under.

2. The word *star* may indicate some other astronomical phenomena than just the normal meaning of *star*.

3. The star apparently moved; it is said to have preceded them.

4. The star also pointed out in some clear manner exactly where Jesus was then living.

5. The star seems to have been lost from sight, for some reason or other, for a period of time. Then the star apparently became visible again.

6. The star does not appear to have been noticed by any one except the Magi. Why?

7. The star contributed in some way to their knowing that the King of the Jews was to be born in Judea.

Besides these peculiarities of the star, certain problems exist concerning the wise men, or more properly speaking, the Magi:

1. The term, *Magi*, originally denoted a group of Medes who acted as Zoroastrian priests for the Persians.

2. Even though Zoroastrianism was monotheistic (originally at least), the term came to denote magicians in general. How? Why?

3. In part, at least, because the term came to denote a profession, it referred to any member of that profession, irrespective of their nationality.

4. The Magi, here and here alone in the Bible, are mentioned favorably. This fact suggests that these Magi were not magicians nor divinators; hence not astrologers. Moreover, the entire account in Matthew does not contain the slightest hint of any astrological meaning. Therefore, these Magi most likely were Zoroastrian priests, probably from Persia. They seem to have watched the heavens, to have considered it and the bodies in it to be the work of the Creator-God.

5. The Magi may have been familiar with Numbers 24:17. This verse, with or without additional information, may have told them of the forthcoming birth of a Jewish prince. They certainly seem to have

been aware that the King of the Jews had been born in Judea; the star which they followed contributed to their knowledge.

Most Bible-believing astronomers have been interested in the exact nature of the astronomical phenomena which produced this unusual star. Several suggestions have been made: meteors and meteorites, comets, novas ("new star"), and conjunctions of planets. Actually none of these completely satisfies the Biblical data or the inferences which can be drawn from them. Consequently many Christians consider the event to be a miracle.

Nevertheless certain conclusions can be reached:

1. The star could not have been a meteor or a meteorite; the life of one is too short.

2. Likewise the star could not have been a comet or a nova without having attracted world-wide attention. Neither seems to have been present at the time of Jesus' birth, although there may be an indication from Chinese records that a nova did appear around this time. While a comet would appear to move, a nova would not.

3. The only remaining possibility is that of the conjunctions of two or more planets. Three times in B.C. 7 (May 29, September 29, and December 4) the planets, Saturn and Jupiter, would appear to come into close conjunction in the constellation of Pisces. This event is comparatively rare, happening only about once every one hundred twenty-five years. Several factors mitigate against this possibility: (1) A closer and similar conjunction happened around B.C. 66. If this kind of conjunction were the cause for the Magian visit, the earlier event, some fifty-nine years before, should also have produced a Magian visit. (2) Another objection to this particular conjunction is that the two planets never seem to approach one another closer than twice the distance of the moon's diameter; therefore they could never have been viewed as a single star. And (3) the difficulty of the star's appearing to be standing over Bethlehem while the Magi were in Jerusalem and

again to be standing there when later they had arrived at Bethlehem (i.e., assuming the star to be a
conjunction of these two planets).

4. Another possibility remains: Early in B.C. 6,
a more unusual event occurred—the conjunction of
three planets—something which happens only about
once every eight centuries. At this time Mars, Jupiter, and Saturn appeared to approach one another
very closely. Some of the objections mentioned in
No. 3 apply here also.

Therefore, although no astronomical phenomenon
can be positively identified as having accounted for
the Star of Bethlehem, the star is definitely not an
astrological event. The star in Matthew, like the
angels and the shepherds in Luke, is used to herald
the great, climactic event of history—the birth of
God's own Son in human flesh and in history to accomplish God's salvation for every person who believes in Him. Therefore, the event glorifies God and
His Son and is the result of His work, whether that
be a miracle or a naturally occurring phenomenon.

Acts 2:9-11

Parthians, Medes, Elamites, dwellers of Mesopotamia, of Judea, Cappadocia, Pontus, and Asia,
Phrygia and Pamphylia, Egypt and the parts of
Libya around Cyrene, visitors from Rome, both Jews
and proselytes, Cretans and Arabs; we hear them
telling in our own languages the excellencies of God.

There have also been those who view the above
verses as presenting nations which are representa-
tive of the twelve signs of the zodiac—thus all the
nations of the zodiac received the gift of the Holy
Spirit. Paulus Alexandrinus, in the late fourth century A.D., provided a list of nations which appear
to be similar in names and sequence to those listed
in Acts, pointing out their astrological significance.
The similarity of names has been exaggerated: only

five of the sixteen in Acts are listed in Paulus—
Cappadocia, Asia, Libya, Egypt (out of sequence in
Paulus), and Cretans. The similarity in sequence
only points out that both Luke and Paulus begin their
list by mentioning nations north of the Fertile Cres-
cent, moving eastward. The probable conclusion is
that Paulus provides us with a list of nations at his
time, while Luke provides us with a list of nations
present on the day of Pentecost—with no further connection between the two lists, and no astrological
meaning in Acts.

Stars and Angels

Throughout history, there have been those who
have seen some connection between stars and angels.[37] This connection can easily be made because
both the stars (Deuteronomy 4:19; II Kings 21:3;
Isaiah 34:4; Jeremiah 8:2; 33:22; and Zephaniah
1:5) and the angels (I Kings 22:19 and Luke 2:13)
are called "the host of heaven" in the Bible. Such
passages as Psalm 148:1-6; and Isaiah 24:21-23; 40:26
have been used to provide the link between two, e.g.,
"It proves that between angels and stars there is
not merely a figurative comparison, but an actual
and real connexion, although one whose details are
still obscure to us." [38] However, in reading these
passages objectively, one discovers that any possible
connection is extremely ambiguous. So, while the
description "the host of heaven" is used of both stars
and angels, it does not mean that stars are angels,
but that the phrase is probably used is Scripture in-
dependently to compare the stars and the angels to
an army. It is also quite possible that in the use of
poetic language, this phrase, "the host of heaven,"
which idolators used to regard the stars as animate,
is used without meaning what they meant by it.

One may also wonder how stars "sing together"

(Job 38:7) and "praise" God (Psalm 148:3), but we must bear in mind that the authors of Scripture often employ poetic language and anthropomorphic terms in connection with these stars. In Job 25:5 we read that "the stars are not pure." Some have seen in this a statement that stars are sinful beings,[39] but in reading the passage we find Bildad the Shuhite speaking, and saying that everything, including the stars, are imperfect when contrasted with God. Thus any support for the stars as animate objects or beings finds very little possible support in the Scriptures.

There are three passages that illustrate the attitude of the prophets in particular and of the entire Old and New Testaments in general toward all aspects of astral worship (Isaiah 47:13; Jeremiah 10:2 and Zephaniah 1:4f.); they condemn its practice unqualifiedly. In fact, as we have seen, there exists no favorable statement concerning astrology, divination in any form, or any kind of pagan worship anywhere in the Scriptures. There is one passage which might be construed to be tolerant of these practices, but, as noted above, it is really in opposition.

Mauder's conclusion concerning astrology is of tremendous import to us today:

> Above all, astrology is an attempt to ascertain the will of God by other means than those which He has appointed—His Son, who is the Way and the Truth and the Life, and His Holy Scriptures in which we learn of Him and which are able to make us "wise unto salvation through faith which is in Christ Jesus" (II Tim. 3:15).[40]

Daniel in the Astrologer's Den

Daniel 1:1—6:27

In the third year of the reign of Jehoiakim, king of Judah, Nebuchadrezzar, king of Babylon, came and laid siege to Jerusalem. The Lord handed Jehoiakim, king of Judah, over to him with a portion of the utensils of God's house, which he took to the land of Shinar, to the house of his god, placing the utensils in his god's treasury.

The king then ordered Ashpenaz, chief of his eunuchs, to bring in for service in his palace some Israelites of the royal family and of the nobility—boys without any defects, goodlooking, versed in various studies, well informed, with intelligent views, fit to take their place in the royal palace— and to teach them the Chaldean literature and language . . .

. . . Among them were from the tribe of Judah, Daniel, Hananiah, Mishael and Azariah, whom the chief of the eunuchs renamed. Daniel he called Belteshazzar, Hananiah Shadrach, Mishael Meshach, and Azariah Abednego . . .

. . . As for these four youths, God gave them mastery and understanding in all the literature and science, and Daniel gained insight in every kind of vision and dream. At the close of the period which the king had fixed to bring them in, the chief of the eunuchs brought them into the presence of Nebuchadrezzar and when the king interviewed them, none among them all were found equal to Daniel, Hananiah, Mishael and Azariah, who therefore entered the king's personal service. On all subjects in which grasp and information counted, the king, as he questioned them, found them ten times more able than all the magicians and astrologers in his entire realm.

In the second year of Nebuchadrezzar's reign Nebuchadrezzar had dreams that disturbed him; he woke up and could not sleep again. So the king gave orders to summon all the magicians, the astrologers, the sorcerers and the Chaldeans to explain to the king his dream. They came and stood in the king's presence, and the king then told them, "I had a dream and my spirit is troubled to know what the dream was." The Chaldeans replied to the king in Aramaic: "O king, live forever! Tell your servants the dream, and we will show its meaning." . . .

. . . The king replied, "I see plainly that you are trying to gain time; because you see how capital punishment awaits you; and that if you do not make the dream known to me there is but one sentence awaiting you. You have banded together to speak false and deceitful words to me, hoping that a change may come. So tell me the dream and I shall know that you can truthfully explain it."

The Chaldeans answered the king, "There is not a man on earth who can tell the king what he asks; for no other king, no matter however great and mighty, has ever demanded such a thing of any magician, enchanter or Chaldean. The king is asking a hard thing, which none can tell him except the gods, whose dwelling is not with mortals." Because of their answer, the king became so angry and furious, that he commanded that all the wise men of Babylon be destroyed. So the decree went forth that all the sages of Babylon should be slain; and they sought Daniel and his companions to slay them . . .

. . . Then Daniel went home and explained the matter to his companions, Hananiah, Mishael and Azariah, that they might ask the God of heaven to be merciful concerning this mystery; and that Daniel and his companions might not perish with the rest of the wise men of Babylon. Then the mystery was revealed to Daniel in a vision of the night, and Daniel blessed the God of heaven, saying: "Blessed be the name of God forever and ever, to whom belong wisdom and might! He changes the times and the seasons; He removes kings and He sets up kings; He gives wisdom to the wise, and knowledge to those who have understanding; He reveals deep and mysterious things; He knows what is in the darkness, for the light dwells with Him. I thank Thee and praise Thee, O God of my fathers; for Thou hast given me wisdom and strength, and hast made known to me what we asked of Thee; for Thou hast made known to us what the king demanded." . . .

. . . The king said to Daniel, whose name was Belteshazzar, "Are you able to make known to me the dream that I have seen, and its meaning?" Daniel answered the king, "No wise men living, be they enchanters, magicians, or astrologers, can tell the king the mystery which the king has asked; but there is a God in the heavens, who reveals mysteries, and He is now about to make known to king Nebuchadrezzar what is to happen in the days to come. Your dream and the visions of your head upon your bed were these: You, O king, as you lay in bed, were thinking of the future, speculating as to what should come to pass hereafter, and He who reveals secrets disclosed to you what is going to happen. As for myself, this secret has not been revealed to me because of any wisdom I possess more than other men, but in order that the meaning may be made known to the king and that you, O king, may understand the thoughts of your own heart.

"You, O King, looked and behold, there stood before you a mighty image, huge and of surpassing brilliancy, and it was terrible to look upon! The head of the image was of fine gold; its breast and arms of silver; its belly and thighs of bronze; its legs of iron and its feet partly of iron and partly of clay. You kept looking at it until you saw a stone, hewn without hands from a mountain, strike the image on its feet of iron and clay, breaking them to pieces—the iron, the clay, the bronze, the silver and the gold, so pulverized that they became like chaff of the summer threshing floor, which the wind carries away, and not a trace of them could be found. But the stone that struck the image became a great mountain and filled the whole earth. Such was the dream; we will now tell the king what it means.

"You, O king, are a king of kings, to whom the God of heaven has given the kingdom, the power, the strength, and the glory, and wherever the sons of men dwell, He has put the beasts of the field, and the birds of the air into your hand, and has given you power over all of them; you are the head of gold! After you another kingdom shall arise, less forceful than you; then a third kingdom of bronze, which shall also have sway over all the earth. And the fourth kingdom shall be as strong as iron; for as iron breaks everything to pieces and beats all things down, so shall it break in pieces and crush all peoples. Yet, as you saw, the feet and toes were partly of potter's clay and partly of iron—and it shall be a divided kingdom; there shall be in it something of the firmness of iron; for as you saw, the toes were partly of iron and partly of clay. So the kingdom shall be partly strong, and partly brittle. As you saw the iron and clay mixed, so shall they be mixed in marriage, but they will not hold together, just as iron does not mix with clay. But in the days of those kings the God of heaven shall set up a kingdom, which shall never be destroyed, nor shall the kingdom be left to another people, a kingdom which shall break in pieces and completely destroy all these kingdoms—it shall stand sovereign forever! And just as you saw that a stone was cut from a mountain by no human hand, and that it broke in pieces the iron, the bronze, the clay, the silver and the gold of the image, so the great God has made known to the king what shall take place hereafter, the dream is certain, and its interpretation sure."

Then king Nebuchadrezzar fell on his face, prostrated himself before Daniel, and ordered that a present and soothing odors be offered to him. The king confessed to Daniel, "Truly your God is the God of gods, the Lord of kings and a revealer of secrets; for you have ably revealed the mystery!" Then the king promoted Daniel, giving him high honors and many large gifts; for he made him ruler over the whole province of Babylon, and appointed him chief governor over all the "wise men" of Babylon. And at Daniel's request, the king set Shadrach, Meshach, and Abednego over the business of the province of Babylon; but Daniel remained a member of the king's court and sat at the main entrance to his palace.

Nebuchadrezzar the king to all peoples, nations, and languages, that dwell in all the earth: "Peace by multiplied to you. It has seemed good to me to show the signs and wonders that the Most High God has wrought toward me. How great are His signs, and how mighty His wonders! His kingdom is an everlasting kingdom, and His dominion endures from generation to generation.

"I, Nebuchadrezzar, was living at ease in my house, and enjoying prosperity in my palace, when I had a dream that troubled me; fancies upon my bed and visions of my head that upset me. So I made a decree that all the wise men of Babylon should be brought before me, that they might make known to me the meaning of the dream. Then came in the magicians, the enchanters, the Chaldeans, and the astrologers; but when I told them the dream, they could not make known to me its message. At last Daniel came in, whose name is Belteshazzar (according to the name of my god) and in whom is the spirit of the holy gods, and I told him the dream saying, Belteshazzar, chief of the magicians, I know that the spirit of the holy gods is in you, and no mystery is any trouble to you; here is the dream which I saw; tell me what it means. The visions of my head which I saw in my bed were these: I looked, and behold a tree stood in the midst of the earth and its height was abnormal! The tree had grown strong until its top reached to heaven, and had become visible to the ends of the whole earth; its leaves were lovely, and its fruit abundant, providing food for all. The beasts of the field and wild animals were sheltered by it; the birds of the air nestled in its branches, and all flesh was fed from it.

"But in the visions of my head on my bed, I looked, and see! a holy guardian, a watcher, came down from heaven and shouted aloud, 'Hew down the tree and cut off its branches; strip off its leaves and scatter its fruit; let the animals flee from under it and the birds fly away out of its branches! But leave the stump of its roots in the earth amid the herbage of the earth with a band of iron and bronze about it. Let the dews of heaven drench him and let him share the herbage of the earth with the animals of the field; let his human mind be taken from him and let an animal mind be given him, and let seven years pass over him. This sentence is by the decree of the Guardian-Watcher and by the authority of the holy ones; in order that all who live may know that the Most High rules the kingdom of men, giving it to whomever He wills and setting up over it the lowliest of men.'

"This dream I, king Nebuchadrezzar saw; and now, you, Belteshazzar, tell me the meaning of it; since all the wise men of my kingdom are unable to make known to me its message; but you are able, because the spirit of the holy gods is in you."

Then Daniel, whose name was Belteshazzar, was stunned and stood aghast for a time, his thoughts appalling him. But the king said, "Belteshazzar, let not the dream and its meaning make you hesitate to tell me." Belteshazzar replied, "My master, may the dream be for those who hate you, and its message for your enemies! The tree which you saw, which grew great and strong, whose height reached to the heavens, and which was visible to the ends of the earth; whose leaves were lovely and whose fruit was plentiful, providing food for all; the tree under which the field animals found shade and in whose branches the birds built their nests—you, O king, are that tree! You have grown and become strong, so that your power has increased till it reaches to heaven, and your dominion extends to the ends of the earth. And as the king saw a watcher, holy one, coming down from heaven and saying, 'Hew down the tree and destroy it; yet save the stump of its roots in the earth, bound about with a band of iron and bronze amid the herbage of the earth, and let him be wet with the dew of the heavens, and let him share with the animals of the field, till seven times pass over him'; this is the interpretation, O king: It is

a decree of the Most High which has come upon my master
the king, that you shall be driven from among men and
you will live as the animals of the field, eating grass like
the ox and wet with the dew of the heavens, till seven years
pass over you and you have learned that the Most High
rules the kingdom of men and gives it to whom He wills.
And as it was commanded to leave the stump of the roots
of the tree, your kingdom shall be assured to you from
the time you learn that it is the Heavens that rule. Therefore, O king, let me counsel you to break off your sins
by practicing justice and showing pity to the oppressed;
perhaps your prosperity may be prolonged."

All this befell king Nebuchadrezzar. At the end of twelve
months he was walking on the roof of his royal palace in
Babylon and the king was saying to himself, "Is not this
great Babylon, that I have built by my mighty power as
a royal residence and for the glory of my majesty?" While
the words were still in the king's mouth, there fell a voice
from heaven, saying, "King Nebuchadrezzar, to you is
this sentence: Your kingdom is taken from you and you
shall be driven from among men; your dwelling shall be
with the field animals; you shall be made to eat grass
like an ox and seven years shall pass over you, till you
learn that the Most High rules the kingdom of men, giving
it to whomever He wills." Instantly the sentence upon king
Nebuchadrezzar was executed. He was driven from among
men, ate grass like an ox, and his body was wet with the
dew from heaven till his hair grew as long as eagles' fea-
thers and his nails as the claws of a bird.

At the end of the days, I Nebuchadrezzar, lifted up my
eyes to the heavens and my reason returned to me. I blessed
the Most High and praised and honored Him, who lives
forever; for His dominion is an everlasting dominion and
His kingdom endures from generation to generation. All
the inhabitants of the earth are accounted as nothing; He
does according to His will in the army of heaven and among
the inhabitants of the earth and none can stay His hand
or say to Him, "What doest Thou?" My reason returned
to me at once and, for the glory of my kingdom, my majesty
and my splendor also returned to me. My counselors and
my rulers came to me for council. I was re-established
in my kingdom and exceptional greatness was added to
me. Now I, Nebuchadrezzar praise, extol, and honor the
King of heaven; for all His works are truth. All His deal-

ings are just, and those who walk in pride He is able to
abase."

King Belshazzar made a great feast for a thousand of
his rulers and drank wine before the thousand. Inflamed
by the taste of wine, he ordered that the vessels of gold
and of silver, which Nebuchadrezzar, his grandfather, had
taken away from the temple at Jerusalem, be brought,
in order that the king and his rulers, his consorts and his
concubines might drink out of them. So they brought in
the golden and silver vessels, which had been taken out
of the temple at Jerusalem and the king and his rulers,
his consorts and his concubines drank out of them. As they
drank the wine, they praised the gods of gold and silver,
bronze, iron, wood, and stone.

Suddenly, that very hour fingers of a man's hand appeared, which wrote on the plaster of the wall of the king's
palace, opposite the lampstand; and the king saw the palm
of the hand as it wrote. The glorious brightness of the king's
face paled and his thoughts alarmed him; the muscles of
his loins loosened and his knees knocked against each other.

The king then called loudly for the enchanters, the
Chaldeans and the fortune-tellers to be brought in. To
them, as the wise men of Babylon, the king said, "Whoever
reads this writing and tells me its meaning shall be clothed
with purple, wear a golden chain about his neck and shall
rank as the third ruler in the kingdom." But when all the
king's wise men came in, they could not read the writing,
nor could any one of them explain to the king its meaning.
At this, king Belshazzar was greatly perplexed; and his
countenance was changed in him, and his rulers were at
their wit's end. Then the queen, because of the cries of
the king and his rulers, came into the banqueting hall, and
the queen said, "O king, live for ever, Let not your fears
alarm you; let not your color vanish! There is in your kingdom one man in whom is the spirit of Deity. In your father's
days there were found in him light, understanding and wisdom like the wisdom of the gods. King Nebuchadrezzar,
your grandfather, made him chief of the magicians, enchanters, Chaldeans, and astrologers; he possessed an excellent spirit, knowledge, and understanding to interpret
dreams, solve riddles, and unravel knots. Call in Daniel;
he will be able to interpret the writing."

So Daniel was brought in before the king, and the king,
addressing Daniel, said: "Are you that Daniel of the exiles

of Judah, whom my grandfather the king brought from Judah? I have heard of you that the spirit of the gods is in you, and that light, understanding and surpassing wisdom are found in you. Already the wise men, the enchanters have been brought in before me, that they might read this writing and make known to me its meaning; but they could not decipher it. But I have heard of you, that you can give explanations and solve problems. Now, if you can read the writing and make known to me its meaning, you shall be clothed with purple, and have a chain of gold to wear around your neck, and shall be the third ruler in the kingdom.''

Then Daniel answered the king, "Keep your gifts, and give your rewards to another; nevertheless I will read the writing to the king and make known to him its meaning. O king, the Most High God gave Nebuchadrezzar, your grandfather, the kingdom with its greatness, glory and majesty: and because of the greatness which He gave him, all peoples, nations and languages trembled and feared before him. Whom he would, he slew, and whom he would, he kept alive; whom he would, he promoted, and whom he would, he demoted. But when his heart became proud and his spirit became haughty and self-confident, he was thrust from his kingly throne and deprived of his glory; he was driven away from human society. His mind was made like the instincts of animals and he lived among the wild donkeys, eating grass like an ox and his body getting wet with the dew of heaven, till he learned that the Most High God rules over the kingdom of men, setting over it whom He wills. And you, his son, Belshazzar, have not humbled yourself, though you knew all this; but you have lifted up yourself against the Lord of heaven; having ordered the sacred vessels of His house to be brought in, that you and your rulers, your wives, and your concubines might drink wine from them. You have praised the gods of silver and gold, bronze, iron, wood, and stone, which can neither see, nor hear, nor understand, and you have not honored God in whose hand is your breath, and to whom belong all your ways.

"It was His palm and His hand which was seen, and it was His writing that was inscribed. This is the writing: 'MENE, MENE, TEKEL, UPHARSIN'. And this is the interpretation of the words: 'MENE'—God has numbered the days of your kingdom and brought it to an end; 'TEKEL'

—you have been weighed in the balances and been found wanting; 'UPHARSIN'—your kingdom is divided and given to the Medes and Persians."

Then Belshazzar gave orders, and Daniel was clothed in purple, a chain of gold was placed about his neck and it was published about him, that he should be the third ruler in the kingdom that very night.

Belshazzar, the king of Chaldea, was slain, and Darius, the Mede, received the kingdom, being then about sixty-two years of age.

It pleased Darius, the Mede, to set over the kingdom a hundred and twenty provincial governors to administer the whole kingdom, and over them three presidents, of whom Daniel was one, so that to them the governors might be responsible and that the king might suffer no loss. Above all the other presidents and governors Daniel distinguished himself, because of his surpassing spirit, so superior that the king was planning to set him over the whole kingdom.

Then the presidents and the governors sought some ground of complaint against Daniel in the discharge of his official duties; but they could find no ground of complaint, because he was faithful, and no error or fault was found in him. So these men said, "We shall find no ground of complaint against this Daniel unless we find it in connection with service to his god."

Whereupon these presidents and governors rushed in jointly to the king, and said to him, "O king Darius, live forever! All the presidents of the kingdom, the chiefs and the governors, the counselors and the rulers have agreed that the king should establish an ordinance and enforce a strict decree, that whoever petitions any god or man for thirty days, except you, O king, shall be cast into the den of lions. Now, O king, lay down the law, and sign it as a document, which cannot be changed forever, according to the law of the Medes and Persians which can not be changed." Therefore king Darius signed such a document in keeping with this decree.

When Daniel learned that such a decree had been officially signed and issued, he went to his house on the roof of which there were chambers with windows opening toward Jerusalem, and three times a day he kneeled and prayed and gave God thanks as he was accustomed to do. Then these accusers came in throngs and found Daniel praying and making humble petition before his God. So they approached the king and reminded him of his decree. They said, "O king! Did you not sign a decree to the effect that any man who prays to any god or man within thirty days except to you, O king, should be cast into the den of lions?" The king replied, "The thing stands fast according to the law of the Medes and Persians, which can not be revoked." Upon this they protested to the king, "That man Daniel, of the exiles of Judah, neither heeds you, O king, nor regards the decree which you have signed; for thrice a day he continues to pray to his own god." When the king heard these words, he was greatly distressed and set his mind to deliver Daniel. He struggled till sunset to rescue him. But these men together rushed to the king, and said, "Know, O king, that a law of the Medes and Persians, in particular a decree of royal authority can not be changed." So the king gave the order and Daniel was aught and cast into the den of lions, the king voicing the hope, "May your God, whom you worship so faithfully, deliver you."

Then a great boulder was brought and laid upon the opening of the den and the king sealed it with his own seal and also with the seal of his rulers, to prevent any possible change of plan about Daniel. Then the king went to his palace, and spent the night in meditation and fasting, instead of enjoying his usual diversions, and his sleep fled from him. In the morning, as soon as it was light, the king arose and went in haste to the den of lions. When he came near to the den where Daniel was, he cried in a tone of anguish and anxiety, "Daniel, servant of the living God, has your God, whom you worship so regularly, been able to save you from the lions?" Daniel answered the king, "O king, live forever! My God sent His angel and shut the lions' mouths and they have not hurt me; because He found me innocent, not having done you any injury."

Then the king was exceeding glad and ordered that Daniel be lifted out of the den. So Daniel was lifted out, and no kind of hurt was found on him, because he had trusted in his God. The king gave orders, and the men who had accused Daniel were brought and cast into the den of lions; they, their children and their wives and before they reached the bottom of the den, the lions overpowered them, and crunched all their bones in pieces.

Then king Darius wrote to all nations, races, and peoples of every tongue that dwell in all the earth: "Peace be mul-

tiplied to you! I make a decree, that in all my dominion
men tremble in reverence before the God of Daniel, for
He is the living God, enduring forever; His kingdom shall
never be destroyed; His dominion shall last to the end;
He saves and He delivers; He works signs and performs
wonders both in heaven and on earth; for it was He who
saved Daniel from the power of the lions."

NOTES

1. Some of these assumptions have been mentioned previously; see chapter 1, pp. 26 ff.

2. For instance, some forms of Buddhism.

3. Hinduism is perhaps the largest and best known of
these faiths.

4. See pp. 78 ff.

5. See chapter 1, especially pp. 19 ff., for the obvious lac
of truth in this statement.

6. For an examination of the meaning of this word and
of its occurrence in the Old Testament see p. 55, Job 38:32.

7. Anderson, Karl, *Astrology and the Old Testament*
(Mokelumne Hill: Health Research, 1965), Facsimile Reprint.

8. Gen. 11:26-25:12; Matt. 3:9; Luke 3:8, 34; John
8:33-40; Rom. 4:1-3, 9-16; Gal. 3:5-9; cf. Ex. 2:24; 3:6, 15f.;
4:5; 6:3, 8; 32:13; 33:1; Lev. 26:42; Num. 32:11; Deut. 1:8;
6:10; 9:5, 27; 29:13; 30:20; 34:4; Jos. 24:2f.; I Kings 18:36;
II Kings 13:23; I Chron. 1:27f.; 34; 16:16; 29:18; II Chron.
20:7; 30:6; Neh. 9:7; Ps. 47:9; 105:6, 9, 42; Isa. 29:22; 41:8;
51:2; 63:16; Jer. 33:26; Ezek. 33:24; Micah 7:20; Matt. 1:1f.,
17; 8:11; Mark 12:26; Luke 1:55, 73; 13:16, 28; 16:23-30;
19:9; 20:37; Acts 3:13, 25; 7:2, 8, 16f., 32; 13:26; Rom. 9:7;
11:1; I Cor. 11:22; Gal. 4:22; Heb. 2:16; 6:13; 7:1-9; 11:8;
James 2:21-23; I Pet. 3:6.

9. Gen. 37:1-50:26; Ex. 1:5-8; 13:19; Num. 1:10, 32; 13:7,
11; 26:28, 37; 27:1; 32:33; 34:23; 36:1, 5, 12; Deut. 27:12;
33:13-16; Jos. 14:4; 16:1-4; 17:1f., 14-17; 18:5, 11; 24:32;
Judg. 1:22f., 35; II Sam. 19:20; I Kings 11:28; I Chron.
2:2; 5:1f.; 7:29; 25:2, 9; Ezra 10:42; Neh. 12:14; Ps. 77:15;
78:67; 80:1; 81:5; 105:17; Ezek. 37:16, 19; 47:13; 48:32;
Amos 5:6, 15; 6:6; Oba. 18; Zech. 10:6; Acts 7:9, 13f., 18;
Heb. 11:21f.; Rev. 7:8.

10. For Jacob and the other patriarchs, see any good
exhaustive concordance.

11. See pp. 51 ff.

12. See pp. 52-55.

13. See pp. 30 ff.

14. Ex. 2:1-Deut. 34:12; Joshua 1:1-7, 13-17; 3:7; 4:10-14; 8:31-35; 9:24; 11:12-23; 12:6; 13:8-15, 21, 24, 29-33; 14:2-11; 17:4, 18:7; 20:2; 21:2, 8; 22:2-9; 23:6; 24:5; Judges 1:20; 3:4; 4:11; I Sam. 12:6, 8; I Kings 2:3; 8:9, 53, 56; II Kings 14:6; 18:4, 6, 12; 21:8; 23:5; I Chron. 6:3, 49; 15:15; 21:29; 22:13; 23:13-15; 26:24; II Chron. 1:3; 5:10; 8:13; 23:18; 24:6, 9; 25:4; 30:16; 33:8; 34:14; 35:6; Ezra 3:2; 6:18; 7:6; Neh. 1:7f.; 8:1, 14; 9:14; 10:29; 13:1; Ps. 77:20; 99 (its title); 103:7; 105:26; 106:16, 23, 32; Jer. 15:1; Dan. 9:11, 13; Micah 6:4; Mal. 4:4; Matt. 8:4; 17:3f.; 19:7f.; 22:24; Mark 1:44; 7:10; 9:4f; 12:19, 26; Luke 2:22; 5:14; 9:30, 33; 16:29, 31; 20:28, 37; 24:27, 44; John 1:17, 45; 3: 14; 5:45f.; 6:32; 7:19, 22f.; 8:5; 9:28f.; Acts 3:22; 6:11, 14; 7:20-37, 40, 44; 13:39; 15:1, 5, 21; 21:21; 26:22; 28:23; Rom. 5:14; 9:15; 10:5, 19; I Cor. 9:9; 10:2; II Cor. 3:7, 13, 15; II Tim. 3:8; Heb. 3:2-5, 16; 7:14; 8:5; 9:19; 11:23f.; 12:21; Jude 9; Rev. 15:3.

15. Num. 22:5-24:25; 31:8, 16; Deut. 23:4f.; Joshua 13:22; 24:9f.; Neh. 13:2; Micah 6:5; II Pet. 2:15; Jude 11; Rev. 2:14.

16. Isa. 1:1-66:24; II Kings 19:1-20:19; II Chron. 26:22; 32:20, 32; Matt. 3:3; 4:14; 8:17; 12:17; 13:14; 15:7; Mark 7:6; Luke 3:4; 4:17; John 1:23; 12:38-41; Acts 8:28, 30; 28:25; Rom. 9:27-29; 10:16-20; 15:12.

17. Ruth 4:17, 22; I Sam. 16:13-I Kings 2:12; *passim.* The references to the word *David* and *David's* are too numerous to list. Please consult a good, exhaustive concordance.

18. See pp. 41, 66-76.

19. For references to other prophets, please consult an exhaustive concordance.

20. See, for example, Isaiah 20:2.

21. See, for example, Ezekiel 4:4-6.

22. *The Jewish Encyclopedia*, II, pp. 241ff.

23. *Loc. cit.*

24. *Ibid.*, pp. 241ff.

25. *Ibid.*, pp. 243ff.

26. In a projected work on the Book of Revelation, the authors will show the utter folly of such a claim.

27. *The Jewish Encyclopedia*, XII, p. 689.

28. For example, Joel 2:10, 31; Rev. 6:12.

29. For example, Rev. 6:13; Isa, 34:4; Acts 19:35; Rev. 8:10.

30. For example, number (Gen. 15:5; Jer. 33:22); height or distance (Prov. 25:3; Job 11:7f.; 22:12; Jer. 31:37; Ps. 103:11); variability in brilliance (I Cor. 15:41); use for calendrical purposes (Job 3:9; 38:7); etc.

31. See, for example Deut. 4:15-19.

32. Ramm, Bernard, *The Christian View of Science and Scripture* (Grand Rapids: Wm. B. Eerdmans, 1955), p. 143. He states that Pinches rejects the mythological reference to Nimrod in this passage as a worthless tradition.

33. Genesis 44:5, 15 are the only strong statements in the Bible to suggest that Joseph or any man of God practiced divination. While it is true that Ancient Near East custom speaks of cups used for the practice of magic, these passages do not explicitly state that Joseph did practice divination, but that the Egyptains and others thought that he did. He certainly excelled their best magicians (Genesis 41:8), but we must note that regardless of whether or not he practiced divination by means of a cup, it in no way proves that he was an astrologer.

34. Stowe, Lyman, *Bible Astrology* (Mokelumne Hill, Calif: Health Research, 1965).

35. Really the twelve tribes of Israel are frequently represented by their prominent ancestors, a son of Jacob, or, in the case of Ephraim or Manasseh, a grandson.

36. In Judaism, there has been found the idea that the stars were animated beings. Some Christian expositors have also held this view. For more information see pp. 62, 63.

37. E.g., Sauer, Erich, *The Dawn of World Redemption* (Grand Rapids: Wm. B. Eerdmans Pub., 1951), pp. 28-29.

38. *Ibid.*, p. 29.

39. E.g., Origin, see p. 81.

40. Maunder, E. W., *"Astrology"*, *The International Standard Bible Encyclopedia* (Grand Rapids: Wm. B. Eerdmans, 1949), I, p. 300.

III

Christianity and Astrology

Originating in the Roman Empire during the first century A.D., Christianity was born into a world of superstition and mysticism in which astrology was given a prominent place. The consultation of horoscopes and omens, the use of amulets and charms, the honor given to astrologers—these were all part of the Greco-Roman world at that time in history. Mystery cults promulgated astrology—Mithraism's votaries invoking the planet ruling the particular day of the week, and the Syrian cult of Atargatis stressing good fortune as guided by the stars and planets.

In general, the atmosphere of superstition prevailed throughout the empire, and, in particular for our study, astrology professed to find in the physical process of the universe the actual controlling powers of life. As such, astrology was a practice and a belief which Christianity had to come to grips with.

The Star in the East

Christianity begins with the birth of Jesus Christ —the Incarnation, the very manifestation in time and space of "God in the flesh"—of which "a star in the east" calls attention to this significant event. Magi, or wise men, came from afar under the guidance of this star to worship Jesus, seeking the one who was born the "King of the Jews." These Magi, then, possibly Jews studying at the astrological school in Sippar, Babylon, may have known of Rabbi Arbarbanel's prediction that when Saturn and Jupiter meet in the constellation of Pisces, the Messiah would be born.[1]

A few years ago scholars deciphered some of the artifacts of the ancient school of astrology at Sippar. Some records found contained some observations which clearly reported the conjunction of these planets (Saturn and Jupiter) in the house of Pisces in 7 B.C. Perhaps this planet conjunction first called attention to the birth of Christ in Judah. Chinese observers later reported comets or supernova in 5 and 4 B.C. These superbright stars, observed as far away as China, may have directed the Magi to Bethlehem where they worshipped Jesus Christ. There is also, of course, the possibility that the star was a miracle, since the star "went before" the wise men and "came to rest over the place where the child was." As such, this would be incapable of scientific explanation.

There is no doubt that some astronomical occurrence called attention to the birth of Jesus Christ, and that it contained an astrological interpretation of great import. But we must remember that it led the Magi to the place of Jesus' birth for the express purpose of worshipping Him.

Judaism

Judaism has no room for astrology in its early history. Being true to the explicit condemnations of astrology in the Prophets, one finds no mention of the practice of astrology or its incorporation in Judaism until the Talmudic period. *The Sibylline Books* praise Judaism because it "does not meditate on the prophecies of the fortune-tellers, magicians, and conjurers, nor practice astrology, nor seek the oracles of the Chaldeans in the stars."

It appears that Judaism and early Christianity did not adopt the practice of astrology from the Chaldeans, but through the syncretistic nature of Hellenism in which some began to practice it. In studying the history and literature of Judaism, one discovers several rabbinical legends attributing astrology to early patriarchs, as well as several parables exhibiting belief in astrology in the Talmud, though the Talmud does contain several condemnations of astrology also. At least one of the Talmudists, Samuel of Babylonia, 250 A.D., practiced astrology, though he did point out that the "Torah can not go together with the art that studies the heavens." By the fourth century A.D., many believed in the influence of the stars at conception and birth and sought guidance from the stars.

During the eighth and ninth centuries, Judaism produced several masters in astrology. In the Cabala we also have mention of astrology, particularly in the Zohar and the Book of Raziel.

Maimonides finally became the authority to strongly oppose astrology, which he believed was bordering on idolatry. He denounced astrology, in his letter to the men of Marseilles, as "a disease, not a science, a tree under the shadow of which all sorts of superstition thrive, and which must be uprooted in order to give way to the tree of knowledge and the tree of life."

Early Christianity

Christianity in the first four centuries was strongly confronted with the problem of astrology. Such eclectic groups as Gnosticism, which adopted certain aspects of Christianity together with Oriental mysteries, Hellenistic philosophy and Babylonian astrology, posed a great problem to early Christianity. Another problem was the fact that astrology was accepted by some within Christianity. For example,

John Chrysostom noted in his *Homilies on First Corinthians* that there were many "in the multitude of our side" who "fortify themselves with their horoscope; many adhere to superstitious observances, and to omens, and auguries, and presages." Christianity, therefore, was required to provide an answer regarding the practice of astrology.

Tertullian, a late second century theologian, stated in his treatise *On Idolatry* concerning astrology: "One proposition I lay down: that those angels, the deserters from God, the lovers of women, were likewise the discoverers of this curious art, on that account also condemned by God." Tactantius, in the fourth century, also stated in *The Divine Institutes* that astrology was the invention of demons. At the Synod of Laodicea in 343-381 A.D. it was declared that " 'Astrologers' are they who divine by the stars through the agency of demons, and place their faith in them."

Because of this belief it was also necessary to make the following declaration: "Those who are of the priesthood, or of the clergy, shall not be magicians, enchanters, mathematicians, or astrologers; nor shall they make what are called amulets which are charms for their own souls. And those who wear such, we command to be cast out of the Church."

Justin Martyr declared in his *Apology* that astrology was "deluded and imposed on by false angels, to whom the lowest part of the world has been put in subjection by the law of God's providence."

There were also those in early Christianity who, like Hippolytus in the early third century, opposed astrology on the grounds that it was irrational and impracticable. Athanasius, the great defender of orthodox Christology in the Arian controversy, wrote of astrologers: "They have fabricated books of tables, in which they shew stars, the which they give the names of Saints. And therein of a truth they have inflicted on themselves a double reproach: those who have written such books, because they have perfected themselves in a lying and contemptible science; and as to the ignorant and simple, they have led them astray by evil thoughts concerning the right faith established in all truth and upright in the presence of God." John Chrysostom in the fourth century in his *Gospel of St. Matthew* wrote, " 'Behold,' say they, 'even when Christ was born a star appeared which is a sign that astrology may be depended on.' How then, if He had His birth according to that law, did He put down astrology, and take away fate, and stop the mouths of demons, and cast out error, and overthrow all such sorcery?"

On the other hand, Origen, writing to his former pupil Gregory in the third century, states: "I would wish that you should take with you . . . as much of Geometry and Astronomy as may be helpful for the interpretation of the Holy Scriptures." Origen also had a very interesting concept of stars. In his *Commentary on John* he notes, "It would surely be absurd to say that He (Jesus) tasted death for human sins and not for any other being besides man which had fallen into sin, as for example the stars. For not even the stars are clean in the eyes of God, as we read in Job, 'The stars are not clean in His sight,' unless this is to be regarded as a hyperbole."

While it is true that there were those in early Christianity who believed in astrology, the prevailent view was to oppose it on the basis that its origin and source of power was from demons and fallen angels. Many early Christians considered scientists as demonologists and immoral when examining them in the light of Christian categories. As Louis MacNeice points out in his book *Astrology,* "The Christians were not opposed to astrology because it was unscientific, but because it was immoral. They tended to think that science was immoral too.''

The Dark Ages

Early in the fifth century Augustine was confronted with the art of astrology. It appears, in reading his *Confessions*, that he was at first attracted to astrology and even dabbled in it. Then later, as he records in his *Confessions*, ''I turned my thoughts to those that are born twins, who generally come out of the womb so near one to another, that the small distance of time between them—how much force soever they may contend that it has in the nature of things, cannot be noted by human observation or be expressed in those figures which the astrologer is to examine that he may pronounce the truth. Nor can they be true; for, looking into the same figures, he must have foretold the same of Esau and Jacob, whereas the same did not happen to them.'' Thus Augustine concluded ''that true predictions made by consulting the stars were not due to skill but to luck, and false ones not to lack of skill but to lack of luck.'' Pope Gregory the Great in the sixth century denounced astrology as false, thus adding his support to the view set forth by Augustine.[2]

It was Augustine's denunciation of astrology as false and erroneous which became the basic position of Christianity during the Dark Ages.

The Middle Ages

Once again astrology came to the forefront. In the eleventh century there was a general revival of neo-Platonism, followed in the twelfth century by a revival of Aristotilian cosmology, which greatly influenced the thought of that period. In the thirteenth century, a Dominican scholar, Thomas Aquinas, utilizing among other sources the astronomical system of Ptolemy and the philosophy and cosmology of Aristotle, produced his monumental work *Summa Theologica*, in which he attributed some characteristics, physique, sex, etc., to the influence of the stars. As John Anthony West and Jan Gerhard Toonder point out in their book *The Case for Astrology*: "The Augustinian objections—entirely valid for their time—were no longer binding; the greatest of the medieval churchmen with almost no exceptions warmly embraced the study of astrology, especially for its symbolic meaning. St. Thomas Aquinas, one of the more hesitant, gave it his blessing only in principle, not in practice."

Back in the eleventh century, Abelard had laid the basic ground work for Aquinas' position and the position of other scholars when he distinguished "naturalia" from "contingentia." Astrology was placed in the realm of "naturalia" in which the stars did influence health, fertility, etc. But this was to be distinguished, however, from the realm of "contingentia" which is dependent totally on God's providence. This distinction was extremely important primarily because those who dabbled in the art of astrology often sought to determine the horoscope of Jesus Christ, but no one wanted to be accused of making God subject to the influence of the heavenly bodies He created. Hildebrand of Bingen did go as far in the twelfth century to state that Christ did choose astrologically favorable moments for the miracles He did while on earth.

An interesting fact of the Middle Ages is that astrologers did enjoy the friendship and support of various popes. Popes Leo III, Sylvester II, Honorius III and Urban V were among those who consulted astrologers, or expressed some interest in this art.

It is important to remember that the position set

forth by Aquinas became the basic view of Christianity during the Middle Ages, recognizing the influence of the stars in certain areas, but always remembering God's providence.

The Renaissance

In the intellectual fervor of the Renaissance astrology once again rose to prominence. Prior to this period of time astrology was always intertwined with astronomy, even though astronomy was concerned almost exclusively with the seven planets in the solar system and their relationship with the earth, while astrology dealt with the signs of the zodiac, the figures which represent twelve of the larger constellations, and their relationship to the affairs of man and earth, much of which resided in superstition. Suffice it to say that up to this time, it was difficult to distinguish between astrology and astronomy, though as early as the seventh century, Isidore of Seville attempted to rid astronomy of astrology.[3]

At the end of the Middle Ages there was a general revival of science, and, in particular, a revival in astronomy. The ancient astronomical system of Ptolemy (Claudius Ptolemaeus), an Alexandrian astronomer of the second century A.D., in which the earth was the center and the sun, moon, and planets revolved about the earth, was soon to be changed.

The event which marked the start of this new cosmology was the publication in 1543 of *De Revolutionibus Orbium Coelestium* by a Polish cleric, Copernicus. In this work he stated that the earth and planets revolved around the sun. Thus Copernicus is the transitional figure in the change to heliocentricity.

Two German Lutherans followed Copernicus. Tycho Brahe, an astronomer, accepted Copernicus' concept of the planets revolving around the sun, but maintained Ptolemy's concept of the sun revolving around the earth. Brahe built a magnificent palace and underground observatory on the island of Hven, filled with tremendous astronomical instruments. His pupil, Johann Kepler, was the one to demonstrate the true nature of celestial movements.

Galileo's observations by means of the telescope which he perfected after its invention in Holland gave great support to the heliocentric view, Isaac Newton, another Christian, founded the theory of universal gravitation, and, as such, tied the universe together in a single system. Newton is a very important figure in the history of astrology. Oliver Lawson points out in his preface to *Aubrey's Brief Lives* that "until the publication of Newton's theory showed the fallacy of the beliefs on which the celestial scheme on horoscopes was founded, astrology had been one of the most serious attempts to explain the world scientifically."

It is interesting to note that while Kepler and Galileo demonstrated the cosmology of Copernicus, they continued to practice certain aspects of astrology which were based upon the ancient Ptolemic cosmology which they rendered obsolete. Both Kepler and Galileo cast some natal horoscopes. It is quite probable that they did so with tongue in cheek, basically to earn a living.

Now a wide gap between astronomy and astrology developed—astronomy basing itself on the heliocentric view of Copernicus, while astrology remained consistent with the geocentric view of Ptolemy. Finally in 1666 the death knell was sounded for astrology: Louis XIV's great minister Jean Baptiste Colbert, on founding the French Academy of Science, expressly forbade astronomers to dabble in the art of astrology.

The Reformation

With a new cosomolgy and a growing distinction between astronomy and astrology, the Reformers sought to discover the answers to new science innovations from the Bible. Luther, in his *Table Talks*, denounces Copernicus' theory: "People give ear to an upstart astrologer who strove to show that the earth revolved, not the heavens or the firmament, the sun and the moon . . . This fool wished to reverse the entire science of astronomy; but sacred Scripture tells us that Joshua commanded the sun to stand still, and not the earth." John Calvin was also in agreement with Luther's position regarding Copernicus.

When it came to the subject of astrology, Calvin denounced it in his *Contre l' Astrologie* as opposed to Christianity. Luther was also opposed to astrology,[4] although he did provide the preface to Johannes Lichtenberger's astrological book in which Luther stated that the heavens gave warning to the godless. The German Reformer Melanchthon, however, was an expert astrologer, and he did occupy the chair of astrology at the University of Wittenburg. Luther had no use for Melanchthon's astrological practices. He wrote, "I have no patience with such stuff. Esau and Jacob were born of the same father and mother, at the same time, and under the same planets, but their nature was wholly different. You should persuade me that astrology is a true science! I was a monk, and grieved my father; I caught the Pope by his hair, and he caught me by mine; I married a runaway nun, and begat children with her. Who saw that in the stars? Who foretold that? Astronomy is very good, astrology is humbug. The example of Esau and Jacob disproves it."

Robert Eisler reports an interesting astrological event regarding Erasmus in his book, *The Royal Art of Astrology.* An Hungarian physician "gave Erasmus an 'astrological' drinking mug shaped like a lion. Having taken his beverage from this vessel for some time, Erasmus felt better, but doubtful whether his improvements were due to its use or not."

We must not forget one of the greatest astrologers of this period and perhaps throughout history, Michel de Notre Dame, or Nostrodamus, who cast horoscopes and made some predictions based on astrology.

The Reformation position which Calvin and Luther formulated denouncing astrology has become the position of Christianity up to the present day.

England

In England astrology prevailed rather strongly in the late sixteenth and early seventeenth centuries. Many influential people participated and indulged in the art of astrology. Even Queen Elizabeth sought astrology, in having astrologer John Dee set the date for her coronation.

At the beginning of the eighteenth century Jonathan Swift dealt a sounding blow to astrology, publishing a bogus forecast entitled *Predictions for the Year 1708, by Isaac Bickerstaff. Written to prevent the people of England from being further imposed on by vulgar Almanack Makers.* By the end of the eighteenth century, astrology was again revived, and a great number of astrological works were published. Several periodicals were also begun, of which *The Prophetic Messenger* is still published today as *Raphael's Almanac, Prophetic Messenger and Weather Guide.* It was in this century that Richard James Morrison founded the Astro-Meteorological Society.

In the beginning of the twentieth century Alan Leo promulgated astrology, publishing *The Astrologer's Magazine*; and in 1920 Charles E. O. Carter founded

The Astrological Lodge of the Society, which issued a quarterly journal *Astrology,* and also offered courses in astrology, granting diplomas to those who completed the course work.

America

The late seventeenth century, eighteenth century, and early nineteenth century saw the birth of many almanacs which were generally based upon astronomy. But astrology came to the forefront in America in the mid-nineteenth century, originating with two non-Christian religious movements, Theosophy and The Rosicrucian Order. It was in 1875 that Madame Blavatsky and Colonel Olcott founded The Theosophical Society, which was later perpetuated by Annie Besant. Rudolph Steiner was also a follower of Theosophy, and his student, Max Heindel, was the one to found The Rosicrucian Order. These two groups, both of which are opposed to historic Christianity, are credited with the origin of the current revival and interest in astrology in America. This, and the present involvement of astrology in the occult, provide us with another theological reason for Christianity's rejection of astrology.

Conclusion

Throughout the history of Christianity there have always been those who pursued astrology; but, for the most part, Christianity has been opposed to astrology on theological and pragmatic grounds. (1) In the first four centuries Christianity generally attributed astrology to the works of demons and fallen angels, and as such, was definitely opposed to astrology. (2) From the fifth to the twelfth century Augustine's view prevailed. Christianity opposed astrology on the grounds that it was false and erroneous, and that it led people astray from Christianity. (3) From the thirteenth to the fifteenth century, the compromise formula of Thomas Aquinas was in practice, in which certain aspects of human affairs were related to the art of astrology. (4) From the sixteenth to the twentieth century the position of John Calvin and Martin Luther prevailed. Christianity opposed astrology as nonsense and incompatible with the Christian faith. The discoveries of many Christian astronomers made void the geocentric basis for astrology, thus further causing opposition to astrology. The fact of the revival of astrology in America originating with two non-Christian religions, and the general intertwining of contemporary astrology with the occult only serve to strengthen the position upon which Christianity has rejected astrology.

Thus, historically, Christianity has been opposed to astrology.

NOTES

1. Finegan, Jack, *Light from the Ancient Past* (Princeton: Princeton University Press, 1946).

2. Gleadow, Rupert, *The Origin of the Zodiac* (New York: Atheneum, 1969), p. 51.

3. *Ibid.*, p. 53

4. Bainton, Roland H., *Here I Stand* (New York: New American Library, 1950), p. 210. Bainton points out one of the reasons why Luther denounced astrology might have been due to the astrologers' predictions of the peasant uprisings, as depicted in a German woodcut of McIntosh, Christopher, *The Astrologers and their Creed* (New York: Praeger Publishers, 1970) p. 95, in which a titlepiece to a German treatise reveals the conjunction of all seven planets in Pisces in 1524 which would cause a peasants' revolt.

IV

The Dawning of the Age of Aquarius

Society is poised on the threshold of a new era, an era of astrological import brought into the focus of our attention in the Broadway play "Hair" by the hit song entitled "Aquarius."

> When the moon is in the seventh house,
> And Jupiter aligns with Mars:
> Then Peace will guide the planets
> And love will steer the stars.
> This is the dawning of the Age of Aquarius.

According to the science of astrology, a new star-age comes into existence approximately every 2,000 years.[1] This occurs when one of the heavenly houses is occupied by one of the signs of the zodiac on the first day of spring, or as others have stated this event, when the sun is computed to enter the first degree of the particular house. This interpretation of history in the light of planetary and precessional cycles was probably first developed by Peter of Abano, and the concept of star-ages is probably a later development of this concept.[2]

Each new star-age supposedly brings with it certain changes: it is generally characterized by new forms of worship, new systems of government, ethics, etc. For example, it has been claimed that during the Age of Taurus, the bull was frequently the object of worship, while in the Age of Aries, the ram was frequently the object of worship. (It should be noted here that while this may be true in some instances and areas, and for certain periods of time, it was not necessarily true in a universal sense.[3])

No one is able to determine precisely the beginning of a new star-age. The Age of Leo is generally dated from 10,000-8,000 B.C., though it has been dated earlier at 10,800. The Age of Cancer is generally dated from 8,000-6,000 B.C., though it too has been dated earlier at 8,640. The Age of Gemini is generally dated from 6,000-4,000 B.C., though it has been dated at 6480. The Age of Taurus is generally dated from 4,000-2,000 B.C., though sometimes dated as beginning 4139 B.C. when it is claimed that the Vernal Equinoctial Point of the northern hemisphere entered the constellation of Taurus. The Age of Aries, generally dated 2000 B.C. to the birth of Christ, is sometimes specifically dated as beginning in 1953 B.C., about the time that the cult of the ram-god Amun began to flourish in Egypt. It has been dated as beginning as late as 500 B.C. The Age of Pisces is the period generally dated from the birth of Christ to the twentieth century, though it has been dated as beginning as late as 1000 A.D.[1]

The Age of Aquarius

Thus the beginning of this new star-age—the Age of Aquarius—is difficult to determine. Some say that it has already begun, while others say it is still futuristic. It has been dated by different individuals as beginning in 1904, 1910, 1917, 1936, and 1962, while such future dates as 2160, 2375, and 3000[5] have also been stated.

This new star-age is proclaimed to be an age of salvation: an age of harmony and peace. It is to be an age of freedom, especially in ethics, in that the ethics of the Judeo-Christian theology and the Puritan morality of the Piscean Age will gradually change. There will also be changes in religion. As Carroll Righter stated: "The Piscean Age was an age of tears and sorrow, focused on the death of Christ. In 1904, we entered the Age of Aquarius, which will be an age of joy, of science and accomplishment, focused on the life of Christ." (From a Christian viewpoint Carroll Righter is incorrect in his judgment of the Piscean Age. Christianity's beginnings focused on Christ's resurrection, and it was the very fact that He conquered death and is alive even today which has empowered Christianity for almost two thousand years.) In *Astrology for the Aquarian Age*, Alexandra Mark has also pointed out that "since Aquarius is known as the sign of universal brotherhood, the church in this new age will strive to make religion more meaningful in terms of man's relationship to men." It should be noted and remembered that all changes in a new star-age develop gradually.

Verna W. Reid points out in her book *Towards Aquarius*: "It was to the coming Age of Aquarius that Jesus referred when he said: 'When the sign of the man shall come he will enlighten you in all things.' " It should be pointed out here that in the Biblical record, Jesus foretells of "the sign of the Son of Man coming," which is a reference to His second coming,[6] and not the "dawning of the Age of Aquarius."

The entire subject of star-ages in which new forms of worship, government, ethics, etc., are introduced through the influence of the planets reveals to us a cyclical view of history.[7] As such the astrologer's view of history as star-ages is distinctly in contrast to the Christian view of history. In each cycle certain aspects are changed under the influence of the stars, but no ultimate goal of history is ever set forth, only for each period. Meaning and purpose are temporary and relativistic, and never set forth in an overall view of history. John Warwick Montgomery succinctly states the Christian view of history in his book *Where*

Is History Going? and reveals the difference in views:

> Let us suppose that historical process were known in its entirety by a God who created both the process and the people who take part in it. Now if this were the case, and if that God entered the human sphere, and revealed to men the origin and goal of the historical drama, the criteria for significance and value in the process, the true nature of the human participants in the drama, and the ethical values appropriate to the process, then, obviously, the question, "Where is history going?" could be sucessfully and meaningfully answered. A gigantic *If*, you say. True, but this is precisely the central contention of the Christian religion: that God *did* enter human life—in the person of Jesus Christ—and *did* reveal to men the nature and significance of history and human life, and *did* bring men into contact with eternal values. "God was in Christ," says the Christian proclamation, "reconciling the world unto himself."

With such a magnanimous concept of history, Christianity has no need for star-ages. God's redemptive plan in the person of Jesus Christ encompasses all ages, and the "hope of the ages" is His return as the sovereign Judge of the universe to consumate the divine plan of the ages.

The Aquarian Gospel of Jesus

According to astrologers, the new age of Aquarius is supposed to bring with it a new religious atmosphere. Some believe that it is only fitting that a new spiritual gospel be composed for this occasion, of which *The Aquarian Gospel of Jesus, the Christ of the Piscean Age*,[8] claims to be the fulfillment.

The author of this "new" gospel is Levi H. Dowling, who was born May 18, 1844, in Belleville, Ohio. Dr. Dowling, who preferred to be known as Levi, served as a chaplain, doctor, Sunday School teacher, and publisher. When Levi was a young boy, he received a revelatory vision in which he was going to "build a white city." This same vision occurred three times in the years following the initial vision.

Levi was a believer in the "Akashic Records, the imperishable records of life preserved in the Supreme Intelligence, or Universal Mind." It is claimed that he spent some forty years in meditation upon these records, attempting to achieve exact accord and harmony of his mind with the Supreme Intelligence. Levi claims that he was able to enter into a conscious recognition of the impressions of the Akashic Records, to collect them, and to translate them with unerring accuracy. The result of this is the written record of Levi's revelatory communication entitled *The Aquarian Gospel of Jesus, the Christ of the Piscean Age.* Levi, believing that this gospel was the fulfillment of the "white city" he was to build, and believing that the Aquarian Age began in 1910, published this work in 1911. Shortly thereafter, he died.

The author has arranged this "new" gospel in sections, chapters, and verses, and under each chapter heading we find a brief summary of the content of that chapter in italics. In general, it is arranged somewhat in the fashion of the King James Version of the Bible—in fact, it is complete with King James English and phraseology.

The work begins with the birth of Mary, and concludes with the sermon of Peter on the day of Pentecost and the beginning of the Church. Much space is given to the life of Jesus, stressing particularly what some refer to as the "lost years of Jesus." One does not have to read far in this work before noticing historical errors. The opening verse "Augustus Caesar reigned and Herod Antipas was ruler in Jerusalem" shatters any hope of historical worth. It is generally accepted that Antipas was ruler in Galilee, but never in Jerusalem. Levi really meant to say Herod the Great. Two verses later we learn that Joachim was the father of Mary, a fact borrowed right out of *The Protevangelium of James.* If the geneology recorded in the Gospel of Luke be that of Mary (which it most probably is), then Mary's father would have been Heli, and not Joachim.

Another interesting facet for those concerned about the historical worth of this "new" gospel is the probability that Levi uses similar names of people (slightly altered) who existed centuries before Jesus, placing them in the period in which Jesus lived. For example, Jesus meets "Meng-ste," the greatest sage of the East, while traveling in Tibet. In the third century B.C. a famous Chinese sage "Meng-tse" lived. Furthermore, John receives his education from an Egyptian priest named Matheno. Again in the third century B.C. we have a famous priest, Manetho.

It is quite apparent in reading this volume to note that several works were incorporated in the formulation of this gospel. First of all, a good part of this work is somewhat a paraphrase of the King James Version of the New Testament. In fact, Levi paraphrases a portion of the last verses of Mark 16 in chapter 180 verses 8-12 which we now know not to have been in the earliest manuscripts we possess of Mark. It is true that in Levi's day they were a part of the King James Version, but today, with the finding of earlier manuscripts, textual criticism doubts the authenticity of that portion of Mark.

One should also note that sometimes Levi changes a quote slightly to reflect a theological bias. Such is the case in quoting John 16:12, 13. In the Bible the "Spirit of Truth" is masculine "he," while in the Aquarian Gospel it reads, "I have many things to say unto you, but you cannot bear them now. Howbeit when *she*, the Spirit of Truth, is come *she* will guide you into all truth." Secondly, Levi makes use of Apocryphal accounts, such as *The Protevangelium of James*, from which he borrowed such events as Mary's birth, Jesus' birth in a cave, and the martyrdom of Zacharias. Thirdly, Levi borrowed from later sources, possibly even from Nicolas Notovitch's *The Unknown Life of Jesus Christ*[9] in which he also speaks of Jesus' visits to the Brahmins, Buddhists and Persians. Fourthly, many of the world's religions have been incorporated, and it would appear that this work is heavily influenced by Gnosticism, Christian Science, and Theosophy.

The concept of God set forth in the Aquarian Gospel reveals the eclecticism of religious tenets which are interwoven into this work. In chapter nine it states:

> Then let us study God, the One, the Three, the Seven. Before the worlds were formed all things were One just Spirit, Universal Breath. And Spirit breathed, and that which was not manifest became the Fire and Thought of heaven, the Father-God, the mother-God. And when the Fire and Thought of heaven in union breathed, their Son, their only son, was born. This son is Love whom men have called the Christ. Men called the Thought of heaven the Holy Breath. And when the Triune God breathed forth, lo, seven Spirits stood before the throne. These are the Elohim, creative spirits of man.

Not only does Levi attempt to provide us with an eclectic view of God, but he also attempts to provide the world with a new religion by making Jesus adept in all that the Oriental religions had to offer. Jesus first studied with Hillel, later with the Brahmins, and Buddhists. In Egypt, Jesus joined the sacred brotherhood and passed through several degrees— Sincerity, Justice, Faith, Philanthropy, Heroism,

Love Divine, and Christ—finally emerging as the Logos. Jesus is made out to preach that "everyone may have this Christ dwell in his soul, as Christ dwells in my soul."

The eclectic and syncretic view of the world's religions presented in this work does injustice to the historical uniqueness and particularistic claims of Christianity. It certainly disregards the testimonies of Jesus and of the primitive church (e.g., John 14:6; Acts 4:12, etc.), and the evidence of the New Testament documents, primary source material, in general. The New Testament declares unequivocally and consistently that Jesus regarded Himself as no less than God in the flesh, and that He received His words, and His wisdom, from God—a view totally foreign to Levi's reconstruction.

The Aquarian Revelations

There are also numerous "revelations" for the Aquarian Age which have come via telethought transmission. Such is the case of messages received from the Space Brothers—our Flying Saucer Missionaries —as revealed to various contactees here on earth. A book *The Aquarian Revelations*, edited by Brad Steiger, presents many of these messages.

From "Outer Space" come the messages of OX-HO to contactees. In one such communication, it was revealed that "the compiling of these messages is like the writing of a gospel for the New Age. . . .The messages which I give you may be called *The Aquarian Revelations*." OX-HO wants his contactees to proclaim "the essence" of his messages, of "peace, love, brotherhood, and beware of coming cataclysms."

From "inner space," we have the scriptures given to man from the Nephli, people who live in deep subterranean caves of this earth. Their revelation is the

Hedon Rogia, the Holy Scriptures of the Cave Masters. (These are claimed to be the original Scriptures, and if they had not been lost, the world would not be in the mess it is in today.) The *Hedon Rogia* begins much like the Bible with the story of creation by the god Tamil. It concludes with the Nephli preparing deep caves, with Tamil revealing to them that they must live there for many ages, until the time of the "New Age." Of course, the *Hedon Rogia* is set forth as secret teachings for that age.

These revelations for the Aquarian Age would call us to look to ambiguous psi-experiences as an experiential base for faith, instead of an empirical grounding on which to base our experience. If, as this book suggests, the *Principles of the Solar Light Center* becomes the creed for the Aquarian Age, we are left with a Cosmic Christ whose invisible second coming is claimed to be synonymous with the starting point of the Age of Aquarius, of the Golden Age; a Jesus of history who was one of several to possess the eternal truths as given by World Avatars. What is even more disturbing is that none of the messages published in this work even mention Jesus Christ at all. In all of this, we find ourselves at odds with the empirical focus of the Biblical affirmation that "God was in Christ, reconciling the world unto himself." We find ourselves denying Jesus as God incarnate and the only Saviour of mankind.

Scripture itself is replete with built-in mechanisms designed as a cumulative safeguard against spurious additives. The original writers were often moved to warn against adding to or taking away from the Word of God, espousing false gospels and revelations, etc. *The Aquarian Gospel of Jesus, the Christ of the Piscean Age* and these other Aquarian revelations appear to be historical violations of these injunctions.

NOTES

1. "The 25,000-year cycle of the Great year, like that of the 360-day year, is divisible into seasons, months, weeks, days and hours. Here we are concerned with its twelve months which correspond to the apparent movement of the sun through the twelve signs of the celestial zodiac. Each great month has a duration of approximately 2,160 years (which will be referred to as two-thousand-year periods), while each of its 360 days measures 72 years of our time or, approximately, the seventy years of man's allotted span of life." Reid, Vera W., *Towards Aquarius* (New York: Arco Publishing Co., 1969), pp. 11 ff.

2. Gleadow, Rupert, *The Origin of the Zodiac* (New York: Atheneum) p. 55.

3. E.g., in the Taurian Age, the main gods in Egypt during the Old Kingdom (2780-2280 B.C.) were Ptah of Memphis and Re, the Sun-god. In Sumer (3500-2500 B.C.), each city devoted its worship to one of the Sumerian deities. In Ur it was the moon-god Nanna and his wife Ningal; in Nippur, Enlil and Ninlil. We do not find the bull as the main symbol of worship in the universal sense which astrology would like it to be.

4. Gleadow, Rupert, *op. cit.*, pp. 55, 171.

5. *Ibid.*

6. C.f. Matthew 24:30 and Luke 21:27 in their context. They explicitly refer to Jesus' Second Coming, even in the Greek text.

7. Reid, Vera W., *op cit.* Chapter 1 especially brings this point out, and the rest of the book bears witness to the cycles of the star-ages.

8. An excellent critique of this book is to be found in Edgar J. Goodspeed's *Famous Biblical Hoaxes* (Grand Rapids: Baker Book House, 1956), pp. 15-19, from which some of the material in this section is presented.

9. *Ibid.*, pp. 3-14.

V

Which Way in Our Day?

Two roads diverged in a wood, and I —
I took the one less travelled by.
And that has made all the difference.
—Robert Frost

Two old faiths, astrology and Christianity, continue today to strive for the allegiance of Western man. Christianity won the first round when the Roman Emperor Constantine accepted Christianity and it became the official religion of the Roman Empire. Since that time Christianity has generally been in the ascending, and astrology frequently has been hard put to survive. But today the situation is quite different! Astrology is on the rise. Christianity, to many people, appears to be dying. Which one will win this final round? Christianity? or astrology? What accounts for the sudden emergence again of the ancient religious superstition (at least that is the way it has appeared historically and still does to modern mankind)? Why hasn't it died a thousand deaths and disappeared like the religions which gave birth to it have done?

Probably the answer to the last question is two-fold. First of all, no one has ever really demonstrated, either from evidence like that produced in courts of justice, or from the scientific viewpoint, that astrology is either valid or invalid. Opponents have been content to ridicule it and to cite objections to it without validating their objections adequately. In a similar manner, practitioners and devotees of astrology alike have made essentially emotional appeals and have cited the evidence of questionable relevance and value. Thus a stalemate has resulted! The time is ripe for an impartial, objective analysis and testing of the astrological data by a person who has adequate astrological training but is not a devotee of the art. This present work is not intended to accomplish this task; neither author meets all the necessary qualifications, although one, when a non-Christian, did study it as well as other occult teachings and did cast and interpret many horoscopes.

The other reason is the failure of Christians to practice their faith and to follow the injunctions of their Saviour and God, Jesus Christ. The scope of this book is not to elaborate on this phase of the problem, only to call attention to its existence. Many essays and larger writings published on the reality, causes, and results of the failure of Christians to be what the name implies have been published.

All that the authors can do is to enumerate some of the fundamentals upon which astrology was erected and make appropriate comments as to their validity. Many of the fundamental assumptions are not considered valid in the Western world, at least, and some of them have been established as being undoubtedly false.

First, large numbers of peoples, from so-called "non-civilized" cultures, like those ancients who prepared the way for astrology, still adhere to the tenets of animism. They have no difficulty in ascribing, as young children do, life to both animate and inanimate objects. They would wholeheartedly agree with the child who stubbed his toe on the stone and then complained to his mother: "That stone hurt my toe! Why did it hit me?"

The aliveness of all nature was connected with breath and could be separated from this natural body, temporarily in sleep, and permanently in death. It is often called *soul*; this use of *soul* must not, however, be confused with its normal usage in Judaeo-Christian and many other ancient and modern writings.

In addition to these two assumptions, ancient man attributed to these "souls" wherever found (stone, plant, animal, or man), the same essential characteristics which they found in themselves. This conviction lies at the root of totemism and other indentifications of a person or group of persons with an animal. It also was one of the basic roots upon which pantheistic concepts were based. In both kinds of religious societies the human or the god is often depicted in animal form (wholly or partially).

Because of these fundamental beliefs, man often added a fourth—the belief that these souls could be transformed from one "organism" to another. The latter found later expression in the religious teachings concerning demon possession and/or obsession, other kinds of personality intrusion (trances, etc.), and reincarnation.[1]

As man became aware of the vaster expanses of creation, he generally transferred these ideas also to the sun, moon, and stars. In time, as we have seen, man deified the mobile celestial bodies and in this manner astral polytheism arose. With the advent of the astral gods, man needed to learn what their will was and what his responsibilities to them were— at least, as a minimum, what man was requested to do in order to have his physical, and growing social and religious, needs satisfied. Consequently, in time he made some further assumptions. Many of these will not be mentioned; only those which are more important in the history of astrology will be noted.

In Mesopotamia, the favorite method of determining the will of the gods was that of hepatoscopy. The assumptions upon which this art of divination was asserted are: (1) The "soul" was primarily located in the liver of those beings possessing one. (2) Whatever god accepted the sacrifice offered to him identified himself with the sacrificial creature. (3) Therefore the liver of the sacrificial animal (i.e., the soul) reflected accurately the will and mind of that god. And finally, (4) Man was able to collect data and learn how to interpret the liver by examining it.

Needless to say the above assumptions have never before proved to be valid nor to be invalid. Men accepted them as self-evident truths for centuries. However, for a long period of time, these beliefs have been rejected, especially by Western man, as being obviously false and as not requiring refutation. These assumptions constituted much of the structure upon which astrology was gradually erected, but they are not essential to it.

The first really important assumption concerning astrology arose from their beliefs in their astral deities who lived in and moved around the celestial skies. They believed that they controlled the history and destiny of mankind. Therefore they gradually assumed that these deities revealed their wills and purposes in the astronomical phenomena. They also began to postulate a one-to-one correspondence between celestial and terrestrial events. These two assumptions underlie, historically, the modern fundamental belief held by most astrological adherents—namely, that some kind of correspondence exists between the stars and human events. This modern restatement does not have to depend upon polytheistic beliefs: it may depend on pantheistic or blend fatalistic concepts. More recently, the underlying roots of this basic idea have been the postulates of humanistic secularism and often of evolution. Some of the meager evidence introduced in its behalf will be mentioned later.

In addition to the secularly stated postulate of astrology, modern-day astrological constructions and the resulting interpretations are still based on the disproven geocentric theory. The emergence of heliocentricity, as a generally accepted fact, destroyed the earlier (and almost universally held) geocentric ideas of mankind. Certainly all astral polytheistic concepts (and seemingly all other viewpoints) of mankind, with the solitary exception of one or two voices like Aristarchus, all very naturally had assumed the apparent self-evident fact that the earth was the center of the universe and that all moving bodies rotated around it. The amazing bit of evidence relevant to this astrological assumption is a negative one—an argument from silence. The destroyers of geocentricity, Copernicus, Kepler, and Newton, do not appear to have suggested that heliocentricity affects astrology in any way.

Perhaps the most startling modern statement concerning the relationship of the geocentric assumption and current-day astrological computations and interpretations is made by one of the better evaluators of astrology, *THE CASE FOR ASTROLOGY* by John Anthony West and Jan Gerhard Toonder. Although they admit that "there are objections that are valid and those that are not," they claim that heliocentricity *was rediscovered* and that the Egyptians, Pythagoreans, Indians, and Chinese all knew the true state of affairs, presumably heliocentricity, and that they all had astrology. These authors, amazingly and without any valid foundation, attribute a knowledge of astronomy to the ancient Egyptians, Indians, and Chinese which cannot be substantiated by the currently available data—all of which points to the universally accepted idea of geocentricity. The earliest known heliocentric theory was proposed in the 3rd century B.C. by Aristarchus; it is true that a Pyth-

agorean, Philolaus (c. 5th or 4th century B.C.), had
proposed that the earth revolved about a central fire.
But he also had the sun, moon, and the planets to
move about this same fire. Hence the Pythagorean
viewpoint was not that of heliocentricity.² Copernicus cites, in addition to these two sources, an old
Egyptian belief that Venus and Mercury revolve
about the sun and thus that the earth is not the sole
center of motion. This idea is not fully heliocentric
because it is also geocentric,³ thus invalidating the
unsupported claims of West and Toonder. Their last
claim needs no additional refutation; as previously
shown, modern astrology is only of Babylonian
origin and dates from about the third century B.C.
The other nations did not have modern astrology, although they did believe in and practice a form of
astrobiology, something which is quite different.

Two additional difficulties confront modern astrologers. These concern the planets: (1) the recent
discovery of the new planets—Uranus, Neptune, and
Pluto; and (2) the fact that astrology, in its origins
and in its history, until comparatively recent at least,
has made no provisions for the possibility that a
planet may be visible for weeks in a row, as, for
example, above the Arctic Circle.

West and Toonder devote about two full pages to
discussing the first problem without really coming
to grips with it. They are undoubtedly correct assuming the validity of astrology, to state that large
scale research is needed in order to ascertain the
meaning of the new planets and how to incorporate
them in the canon. At the moment, the existence of
these planets presents a real problem to traditional
astrology.

The second difficulty is ignored by astrologers;
above sixty-six degrees latitude, it is virtually im-
possible to calculate what zodiacal point is rising

on the horizon. Since this computation is essential
to the construction of a horoscope, no valid one can
be made for those born in Alaska, northern Canada,
Greenland, Norway, Sweden, Finland, Siberia, and
other Arctic regions. For them there can be no celestial influences to determine their lives[4]—a ridiculous
situation!—that is, if astrology is true!

Other objections include the contention that there
can be no action at the distance required by the sun
and planets on mankind, especially considering the
composition of these material bodies. Behind this objection lies the assumption, implicit in those already
stated, that the solar system and its components constitute an organism or a group of interrelated or-
ganisms. The planets, as West and Toonder state,
may be viewed as functions of the organism, i.e.,
the solar system itself. In other words, the solar system and its components possess consciousness and
will. Admittedly this assumption has never been established, but neither has its opposite, the position
taken today by Western and related cultures. Moreover, it is difficult to conceive of inaminate objects
as possessing consciousness and will unless a person
presupposes certain pantheistic or polytheistic beliefs.

A valid objection to astrology is that it does not,
usually at least, base its horoscopic constructions and
interpretations upon valid data. Part of this objection
has previously been mentioned concerning the geocentricity of the astrological horoscope. More pertinent are the facts that the equinox no longer is
the same as it was some 2000-2500 years ago. The
sun does not appear to rise at 0^0 of the constellation
of Aries, but has moved to about 7^0 of Pisces. Thus
a person born on the twenty-fourth of October should
show for his astrological sign Libra and not Scorpio.
Which is he? A Scorpian? or a Librian?

The problem is not new. It has been recognized for centuries. Interestingly there does exist today a small, vocal group of astrologers who insist that the sidereal zodiac (i.e., the one which moves) is the only correct one. They have tried to establish their argument by statistical studies. Most astrologers, however (the conventional ones), maintain that the statistical data may be construed in a variety of ways and "that their own collective experience testifies to the validity of the standard tropical zodiac." West and Toonder make some suggestions on how the two concepts may be reconciled.

Probably much more pertinent is the relationship of heredity and time and place of birth. The important biological point in the history of each individual is not the time and place of birth, but the act of conception. This problem has been recognized for centuries. Ptolemy was aware of this, but he finally rationalized the difficulty. The books, *Hermes Trismegistus*, have, even in their fragments, elaborate rules for determining the moment of conception. In other words, ancient astrologers recognized the problem and attempted to deal with it. Actually there is an approximate correlation between that of birth and that of conception; moreover, in the past (and even now usually) the place of conception and the place of birth were one and the same or so nearly the same as to constitute a negligible factor. Today this is not always true; persons conceived at one place may be born thousands of miles distant from that place. Moreover, the relation between conception and birth is not only complicated by the many variables concerning birth (natural and induced premature births, as well as delayed births) but also by the increased uncertainty as to the time of conception. It may occur as much as twenty-four hours after the sexual act. Except for these unknown factors; the normal

time span between conception and birth may only
mean that, instead of speaking of a person being born
under the sign of Scorpio, one should speak of him
as being conceived under the sign of Pisces—with
appropriate reallocation of the interpretative data.

Of course for the astrologer who is a reincarna-
tionist the problem may be somewhat different. His
difficulty lies in ascertaining with certainty the time
when the "soul" enters the body; it may be any time
from conception to shortly after birth.

In addition, one more fact needs to be stated. The
concept of heredity itself is no longer as simple as
it has recently appeared to be. The genes, DNA, are
no longer definitely the sole factor in heredity; some
scientific evidence has been uncovered to suggest the
possibility that factors outside the genes may control the genes and influence the biological inheritance
of an organism.

In this context at least two other difficulties must
be mentioned: time-twins and physical, identical,
and fraternal twins. On either the astrological or the
physical hereditarial basis, identical twins present
no problems. The difficulties lie with time-twins and
fraternal twins. Insufficient, fully and unquestionably
established data is available to pass judgment on
time-twins which are not fraternal twins. Such meager data as supplied by astrologers or their followers
suggests only the possibility that such exist and that
they are essentially "identical" in their astrological
futures. But since fraternal twins are definitely born
at the same place and normally are born very close
in time to one another, there should be a close correlation between their astrological futures. Such correlation, however, does not exist. Therefore a real
problem exists—one which usually cannot be accounted for by the short interval of time. The "con-
ceptional astrologer" is in a better position because

he can maintain a longer time differential for the two conceptions than the "birth astrologers" can for birth.

The problem of postponed and premature births require the conventional astrology to insist (as it does) that these births make considerable difference in the character, etc., of the child. Who can prove that they are wrong? But also, who can establish that they are right?

A much more difficult situation concerns the mass tragedies—the Jews and Christians massacred by Hitler; the Japanese killed by the atomic bomb, the soldiers (and civilians) killed in World War II as a result of bombing, etc. This difficulty has been brought up and considered by astrologers. At its roots lie the inability of the astrologer to distinguish completely and satisfactorily the general and the particular. The astrologer maintains that the destiny of an individual must be considered as operating under the greater laws which control his city, state, nation, or race. Men, even before astrology arose, engaged in this art of astrology, and in this area they still persist even though they no longer have an adequate basis for accounting for the differences between races, between regions, between nations, or even between neighboring communities. The assembly of gods, where each god had a particular area assigned to him in the heavens and on the earth, exists no longer in the imaginations of modern men. There may exist intriguing studies which pertain to aspects of this area.

A great deal of the last objection which West and Toonder state has already been discussed. There is no doubt that much of the zodiac used by astrologers is purely arbitrary and corresponds to nothing whatsoever in objective reality. This objection therefore, stated in this manner, is very crucial. For astrologers to establish their position, conclusive evidence must be produced, and they must produce it. It does not suffice to insist that astrology sounds reasonable or for example that, by astrology, the moon's (and/or the sun's) influence upon the tide suggests a similar influence upon human beings. Perhaps the ignoring of most, if not all, of the pertinent astronomical, biological, and other relevant scientific data by astrology in their calculations and interpretations should be mentioned in this connection. These factors remove astrology from the area of rationality for vast numbers of modern man and reduce it in conception to an outmoded, disproved relic of the age of magic. Certainly until such relevant evidence of its validity, and until the attitudes of astrologers change toward scientifically established data, intelligent persons will continue to have no part or parcel of it.

In concluding, a few more relevant matters need to be considered. One concerns a question, stated earlier, but not yet answered. It can be profitably restated again: In view of the questionable case for astrology, how does it happen that, even in Western, traditionally Christian, culture astrology has gained such popularity?

There are at least three characteristics of our present age which account for the decline of the influence of Christianity and the appeal of astrology for modern man; these characteristics have been true of each previous age in which astrology was on the ascendency. The first, and undoubtedly the most important, is the rejection of God by modern man. Ever since the Renaissance, mankind in the West has been moving toward secularism and humanism and away from a belief in and a dependence upon God. This tendency has been accelerating during the past two-three centuries, especially since the time of Darwin. In this post-Darwinian period, man has rejected God in ever increasing numbers. Needless to say, this trait in mankind also characterized the age in which astrology rose to its zenith in Babylon, and the age when it was accepted and embraced by the Greeks, the Romans, and the Egyptians. In fact, it was true when the roots of astrology was born and astrobiology emerged. Even the Middle Ages, the one period of Christian history when astrology flourished, was a period characterized by its godless, immoral life.

A second characteristic of these periods is the filling of these voids or vacuums by some false god or gods. In the post-Darwinian era that vacuum was filled by science and its high priests, the scientists. To Western man science seemed to have all the answers to man's questions and problems—past, present, or future. This increasing acceleration of humanism has continued, until, as Jung has discovered, the area within man formerly filled by God and religious ideas is now filled with the symbols of man himself. In the former periods the decline in the older worship of the gods was filled by the worship of new gods, e.g. the oriental mystery religions which became so popular in the Graeco-Roman world and the rise of polytheism after the rejection of the true God. The latter, as we have seen, eventually gave rise to astrobiology and eventually to astrology itself.

Unfortunately man in our age, just as in previous ages, failed to realize the meaninglessness and the purposelesness which is found in humanism and which has been so well stated by J. B. Phillips in his book, *Making Men Whole*:

> Let us, the humanist says in effect, work for the good of mankind, teaching, healing, improving. We shall always be "working for posterity," but that is a fine unselfish thing to do and we must not mind that. Very well then, let us assume that this fine work is successful and that in the remote future the human beings then living on this planet will have conquered

nature by scientific knowledge. All tensions and mal-
adjustments of personality will have been removed
by vastly improved psychological methods, and men
and women will be unbelievably healthy, wealthy and
wise. But, what after that? This planet will eventually cease to be able to support life or will be destroyed by collision with another celestial body. This
means that the sum total of human progress, of every
effort and aspiration and ideal will be annihilation
in the deathly cold of inter-stellar space. *And there
is nothing more to come.* Of course if we stop short
of the final scene they may persuade themselves that
the eventual happiness of our descendants a million
years hence is a worthy ideal for which to live and
die. But if the end of all is *nothing, sheer non-exis-
tence,* surely no one but a fool can call that an ideal
worthy of his adult allegiance.

Eventually, especially in the past two or three
decades, man has become disillusioned by and dis-
enchanted with the god he had created—himself or
as he called it, science. He has realized the futility
and the inability of science to satisfy his needs,
his aspirations, and his difficulties. Thus he is in a
real quandary; he no longer recognizes the real true
deity of the universe, the God of the Judaeo-Christian
Scriptures. Moreover, having discovered the inade-
quacy of his manufactured god, he again has a vacuum. *But this time there is nothing to fill it.*

Hence, he just drifts and expresses his melancholy
and hopelessness in a variety of ways. Two of the
more noticeable and vocal ways are: (1) the many
rebellions which are occurring in all parts of the
world, but especially in the West and those portions
most influenced by Western ideas; and (2) in the rise
of modern cults and the revitalizations of older religious superstitions, such as astrology. This feature
also was so very true of the prior ages in which astrology flourished. In each of these ages man has
demonstrated the truth of Paul's statement:

Therefore God gave them up in agreement with their inner cravings to such impurity as dishonored their own bodies, since they altered God's truth into falsehood, and revered and served the creature rather than the Creator, who is blessed forever. Amen. For this reason God abandoned them to shameful passions.... Just as they did not care to acknowledge God any more, so God gave them over to subverted tendencies, to practice what is not decent, until they are full of every sort of wickedness, immorality, depravity and greed; crammed with envy, murder, quarreling, deceit and malignity.

—Romans 1:24-26a, 28-29

Unfortunately man still has not learned that all he needs to do is to turn to the Creator: because, as Jesus said, "I will certainly not cast out anyone who comes to Me"; and "whoever believes in Him should not perish, but have everlasting life."

In view of the essentially negative attitude, and of the nature of the conclusions thus far expressed regarding astrology, does any evidence exist favorably inclined toward it? The answer is *yes*. Yet even this affirmative answer requires considerably more qualifying than astrologers or those, like West and Toonder, are willing to acknowledge. In the third part of *The Case for Astrology*, West and Toonder adduce and restate a considerable mass of investigations which may indicate that "there is something in astrology." The evidence is not all of equal value of relevance. Much of it is difficult to verify—i.e., it can not be subjugated to scientific tests of truth or validity. A good deal is statistical evidence which, like all statistical data, requires the most careful scrutiny in order to be sure that the data favors the conclusions which have been alleged. The investigators range from psychologists, like Carl Jung, on to statisticians, philosophers (originally a member of the theosophic group), electrical engineers, astrologers, and the like. All sorts of data involving radio disturbance, the influence of the moon on living organism, to the correlation of data in the birth horoscopes with their future occupations and the like, are presented.

One of these investigations presents rather intriguing results. A French graduate in statistics, Michael Gauquelin, sets out to disprove the claims of astrologers (according to West and Toonder). The results of his studies are available in English in two works, *The Cosmic Clocks* and *The Scientific Basis of Astrology*. The latter has the subtitle *Myth or Reality*. His conclusions are rather mixed. He finds that traditional astrology is invalid. It is a mass of logical contradictions and has erred in attempting to explain cosmic actions in terms of occult characteristics, which the heavenly bodies obviously cannot possess.

Gauquelin, on the other hand, does point out that "amazing links relate man to the sun" and that our surrounding cosmos is neither changeless nor void. He believes that new phenomena has been (or is in the process of being) discovered. In *The Cosmic Clocks* he calls this new discovery "planetary heredity." In *The Scientific Basis of Astrology* he traces the origin of his interest in and bias toward astrology, the history of astrology, and his own investigations. The latter, he concludes, establish certain astrological claims—e.g., "a correlation between the birth of shy parents with that of their children," and also one between that of an individual and of his future occupation. He concludes with the idea that a new science is being born, and with its birth also associates A. L. Tchijewky (Russian), H. Bortels (German?), Maki Takata (Japanese), G. Piccordi (Italy), and A. Brown (USA).

There is no corrobative evidence that these men

agree with Gauquelin in being instrumental, along with him, in the birth of this new science. On the other hand, West and Toonder are hardly correct in stating that he has quantitively established an ancient astrological tenet that the positions in the birth horoscope of the planets bear a meaningful relationship to one another. They further suggest that he is destined to be recorded in history as *L'Astrologue Malgré Lui*. Perhaps so, in histories of astrology written by astrologers and by their devotees. In objectively written histories he will be recorded, unless he changes radically his position in the future, as the greatest scientific opponent of traditional astrology, or at least as one of the greatest modern opponents.

Therefore, in conclusion, *The Case for Astrology* has not been established. No meaningful evidence exists to establish a case for it in its ancient form. As Gauquelin has so aptly stated, no essential difference exists between a modern horoscope and its interpretation and one made twenty centuries ago. This fact, of course, does not prove the falsity of this variety of divination. In all fairness, another conclusion must also be stated: *The Case Against Astrology* has not been proved. The most that can be said at this time is that the astrological theory concerning the arbitrary theoretical but non-existent (insofar as objective reality is concerned) relationship of the "stars" in a birth horoscope *may mask* a scientific reality. If it does cover up such a reality or truth, that reality or truth has not yet been established or clearly formulated.

Using Frost's figure of speech, modern man is traveling and two roads are open to him. Which road will he choose? The road of mysticism, magic, divination, and astrology, or the path of truth which leads to freedom and which gives man his real needs

and desires—the path of the true Creator God, and
of Jesus Christ. This is the area of "ultimate concern"—the concern with which all of us must face
and come to grips. Ultimately we all place our trust
in something or someone—man, astrology, or God.

If we place our ultimate in man, we really have
no need for astrology or God. We are left in the work-
ing of fate which has been presented over and over
again in the theatre of Beckett, Pinter, and Hoch-
hurth, as well as in the art, literature, music, and
other media which illustrate and depict the despair
of modern man.

But to place our ultimate trust in astrology is
equally as despairing. If astrology be our guide, we
have no need for God or any hope for man. Robert
Eisler points out in his book *The Royal Art of Astrology* that astrology is a "superstitious residue of
what was once a great, pantheistic religion and a
glorious philosophical attempt to understand and
rationally to explain the universe." As such we are
faced with the universe as a single, all-embracing
unity, a mechanistic closed system without real purpose, meaning, or ultimate goal. We have no doubt
today that the universe exists, and by pronouncing
it worthy of our ultimate trust and giving it the title
"God," we explain absolutely nothing, nor do we
solve the predicament we find ourselves in today.

Christianity presents the solution to the dilemma
of modern man—God. He created the stars, planets,
sun, moon; created man in His image for a purpose;
loves man and entered the universe as man in the
person of Jesus Christ to deliver him from despair;
and presents direction and ultimate goal for history.

As Isaiah the prophet noted over 2600 years ago:

> You have spent weary hours with your many
> advisers. Let them come forward now and save you,
> those who analyze the heavens, who study the stars

and announce month by month what will happen to you next. . . .

This is what your wizards will be for you, those men for whom you have worn yourself out since your youth. They will all go off, each his own way, powerless to save you.

The answer is not to be found in the stars or with man, but in Jesus Christ, as He is revealed in the Bible.

Two roads diverged in a wood, and I—
I took the one less travelled by.
And that has made all the difference.

—Robert Frost

Which road do you choose to take? It will make all the difference to you for the rest of your life!

NOTES

1. See the forth-coming projected work of these authors on this subject.

2. Berry, *A Short History of Astronomy*, p. 25.

3. *Ibid.*, p. 99.

4. Gauquelin, *The Cosmic Clocks*, p. 84.

BIBLIOGRAPHY

Adams, Evangeline, *Astrology: Your Place Among the Stars,* New York: Dodd, 1930.

Allen, Don C., *Star-crossed Renaissance,* New York: Octagon, 1966.

Anderson, Karl, *Astrology of the Old Testament* (Facsimile Reprint), Mokelumne Hill: Health Research, 1965.

Berry, Arthur, *A Short History of Astronomy,* New York: Dover, 1961.

Bullinger, E. W., *The Witness of the Stars,* London, 1894.

Cohen, Daniel, *Myths of the Space Age,* New York: Dodd, Mead, and Co., 1967

Cramer, F. H., *Astrology in Roman Law and Politics,* New York: American Philosophical Soc., 1954.

Cumont, Franz, *Astrology and Religions Among the Greeks and Romans,* New York: Dover, 1912.

Dampier, W. C., *A History of Science,* London: Cambridge University Press, 1966.

DeCamp, E. Sprauge, and Catherine C., *Spirits, Stars, and Spells,* New York: Canaveral Press, 1966.

Eisler, Robert, *The Royal Art of Astrology,* London, 1946.

Fazan, C., *Zodiacs Old and New,* London, 1931.

Gammon, Magaret H., *Astrology and the Edgar Cayce Readings,* Virginia Beach: A.R.E., 1967.

Gauquelin, Michael, *The Cosmic Clocks,* New York: Avon, 1969.

Gauquelin, Michael, *The Scientific Basis of Astrology,* New York: Stein & Day, 1969.

Gleadow, Rupert, *The Origin of the Zodiac,* New York: Atheneum, 1969.

Goodavage, Joseph F., *Astrology: The Space Age Science,* New York: New American Library, 1967.

Graubard, M. A., *Astrology and Alchemy; two fossil sciences,* Phila: Philosophical Library, 1953.

Hawkes, Jacquetta, *Man and the Sun,* London, 1963.

Heindel, Max, *Message of the Stars,* San Jose: Rosicrucian, 1966.

Howe, Ellic, *Astrology*, New York: Walker and Co., 1968 (originally published in England as *Urania's Children*).

Jocelyn, John, *Meditations on the Signs of the Zodiac*, San Antonio: Naylor Co., 1966.

Levi, *The Aquarian Gospel of Jesus the Christ*, Los Angeles: De Varss and Co., 1964.

MacNeice, Louis, *Astrology*, New York: Doubleday, 1964.

Maunder, E. W., *Astronomy of the Bible*, London, 1909.

McIntosh, Christopher, *The Astrologers and Their Creed*, New York: Frederick Praeger, 1969.

Montgomery, John Warwick, "Cross, Constellation, and Crucible: Lutheran Astrology and Alchemy in the Age of the Reformation", *Ambix, the Journal of the Society for the Study of Alchemy and Early Chemistry*, XI, 2, 65-85.

Neugebauer, Otto, *The Exact Sciences in Antiquity* (Second Edition), New York: Harper & Row.

Parker, Richard A., *The Calendars of Ancient Egypt*, Chicago, 1950.

Redi, Vera, *Towards Aquarius*, New York: Arco, 1969.

Rolleston, Frances, *Mazzaroth*, London, 1862.

Sachs, A., "Babylonian Horoscopes,"—*Journal of Cuneiform Studies*, VI, 2, 54-57.

Sarton, George, *A History of Science*, New York: John Wiley & Sons, 1964.

Steiger, Brad (Ed), *The Aquarian Revelations*, New York: Dell, 1971.

Stowe, Lyman E., *Stowe's Bible Astrology* (Fascimile Reprint), Mokelumne Hill: Health Research, 1965.

Webb, E. J., *The Names of the Stars*, London, 1952.

West, John Anthony, and Toonder, Jan Gerhard, *The Case for Astrology*, New York: Coward-McCann, 1970.